Sermons on the Parable of the Sower
by Edward Harwood

S E R M O N S

ON THE

PARABLE of the SOWER.

Seminis modo fpargenda funt, quod quamvis fit exiguum, cùm occupavit idoneum locum, vires fuas explicat, et ex minimo in maximos auctus diffunditur.　　SENECÆ Opera, p. 134.
　　　　　　　　　　　　　　Edit. Gronovii. 1672.

SERMONS

ON THE

PARABLE OF THE SOWER.

BY

E. HARWOOD, D.D.

LONDON;

Printed for JOSEPH JOHNSON, No. 72, Saint Paul's
Church-yard.   1776.

TO

THE REVEREND

PHILIP FURNEAUX, D. D.

IN TESTIMONY OF

HIS LEARNING AND ABILITIES,

AND IN COMMEMORATION OF LONG

ESTEEM AND FRIENDSHIP,

THESE SERMONS

ON THE PARABLE OF THE SOWER

ARE INSCRIBED

BY HIS SINCERE FRIEND AND OBLIGED SERVANT,

EDWARD HARWOOD.

PREFACE.

THE following Set of Sermons was originally written in Bristol, and preached to a small Church in that City. The favourable acceptance they met with, and the greatness of the Object I had in view when I composed them, have encouraged me to deliver them to the Public. I wrote them with this design : To instruct and edify my Auditors, and to evince the Character of Jesus Christ as a Divine Moralist, from his perfect knowledge of the human heart, and his accurate descriptions of a variety of characters.

E. Harwood.

Great Russel Street,
Bloomsbury, London,
    May 16, 1776.

The PARABLE of the SOWER.

MATTH. XIII. 3——9.

And he spake many things unto them in parables, saying, Behold, a Sower went forth to sow : and when he sowed, some seeds fell by the way-side, and the fowls came and devoured them. Some fell upon rocky places, where they had not much earth ; and forthwith they sprang up, because they had no deepness of earth. And when the sun was up, they were scorched, and because they had not root, they withered away. And some fell among thorns, and the thorns sprang up and choaked them. But others fell into good ground, and brought forth fruit, some a hundred-fold, some sixty, some thirty-fold. He that hath ears to hear, let him hear.

SERMON I.

MATTH. xiii. 3.

And he spake many things to them in parables, saying, Behold, a Sower went forth to sow.

THE Evangelist introduces this instructive apologue with observing, that parable was the usual vehicle, in which our Lord conveyed his doctrines to the multitude. *He spake many things to them in parables* It was the best method of communicating instruction he

B   could

could have chofen.   For thefe concife
moral ftories would make indelible
impreffions upon the minds of his
audience.   They would be infinitely
better remembered, be more eafily
recollected, than all the beft didactic
precepts of a formal morality. The memory for ever retains a fhort inftructive moral hiftory, while philofophic
reafoning and fpeculative argumen-
tation, however juft and agreeable
when we heard them, are foon loft to
our remembrance.

Befides, this method of teaching by
parable was not only the happieft
that could have been felected, but
it was the fafeft.   Had our Lord
communicated his doctrines in an
open undifguifed manner, and without referve affured them, that he
was the heavenly Inftructor, whom
God had repeatedly promifed to the
world—that he was the great Meffiah
and

I

and Lawgiver of mankind—and they muſt receive theſe truths as the doctrines and diſcoveries brought from heaven to men by this commiſſioned Inſtructor: the conſequence of theſe open and avowed declarations would have been, that the Jewiſh nation would unanimouſly have made him King—diſcarded immediately all ſubjection to the Romans—would have erected that temporal kingdom under the Meſſiah, which had been ſo long the object of their fondeſt expectations: conſequently this rebellion would have given umbrage to imperial Rome, who would by force of arms have attempted to recover a loſt province—every thing would immediately have been thrown into infinite confuſion, the death of the Meſſiah would have been accelerated, the prophecies would have been defeated, the great ends of his coming fruſtrated, and, without a ſpecial interpoſi-

tion

tion of Providence, all the fpiritual bleffings of the Meffiah's kingdom would have vanifhed for ever. Our Lord therefore, to prevent what one of the Evangelifts tells us, *the people's taking him by force, and making him a King*, veiled his facred truths in the pleafing fhade of moral fable and fiction. One of the writers of his life affures us, that *without a parable be never fpake* to his audience. It was his cuftomary and uniform method of inftruction. It was the fafeft in the prefent fituation of things, and it was the propereft and beft adapted to the moral ftate and difpofition of his hearers. For all the virtuous and well-difpofed, thofe who came folely with a view to grow wifer and better, would clearly un-derftand thefe Parables, would clearly fee the heavenly truths they couched: while they would be entirely loft upon all who came merely out of curiofity,

or

or with all their Jewish prejudices and bad dispositions about them.

Moreover, public instruction by Parables was attended with another happy advantage with respect to the hearer. It would immoveably fix his attention. All the time of the recital his sagacity and penetration would be employed to unravel the fable, and find out its great moral. It was paying a compliment to the understanding of the Auditor, in supposing him capable, by the exercise of his abilities, of discovering the latent truths, and seeing through the artful interposing shade.

With what fixed, eager attention may we justly suppose the innumerable crowds must listen to these Parables! With what inexpressible ardour must they hang on the lips of the Divine Speaker! While our Lord

B 3.   was

was delivering thefe Parables with an
air, and dignity, and folemnity, that
befpoke his miffion from God, all
thefe vaft immenfe crowds would be
all ear, all attention. All would be
hufhed and loft in thought—one ftill,
filent fcene, not difturbed by a word,
hardly interrupted by a breath. With
what avidity may we conceive them
fufpended on his inftructive accents,
and imbibing the truths that flowed
from his facred lips—eager not to
lofe a fingle ftep, a fingle word of the
Parable—all their faculties and powers all the while in vigorous glowing
exercife, to explore the meaning he
intended, and difcover the moral he
defigned to convey.

I cannot enter upon the explication
of this Parable of the Sower, without making another remark. This relates to the *place* and *manner* in which
our Saviour delivered it—and you
will

will agree with me, that the *scene* and *place*, both for *hearing*, and for *speaking* to such an infinite number of people as were then assembled, was the happiest possible. Our Lord went into a boat, and the multitudes formed themselves upon the rising beach. The regular declivity of the shore would have the appearance, and the same convenience for seeing and hearing, as the sloping seats of an Amphitheatre. — Almost every one, by the advantage of the ground, might *see* him, and *bear* him, as he discoursed to them from the ship on the lake below them.

When they were all convened together in one vast assembly — one rank uniformly above another — all fixed in the most deep and profound attention — he addressed himself to them in the following manner:

*Behold a Sower went forth to sow:
and when he sowed, some seeds fell by
the way-side, and the fowls came and
devoured them. Some fell upon rocky
places, where they had not much earth,
and forthwith they sprang up, because
they had no deepness of earth. And
when the sun was up, they were scorched; and because they had not root, they
withered away. And some fell among
thorns, and the thorns sprang up and
choaked them. But others fell into good
ground, and brought forth fruit, some
a hundred-fold, some sixty, some thirty-
fold. He that hath ears to hear, let
him hear.*

I intend to make some reflections
on the several parts of this instructive
Parable, in the order they occur, and
beg of God, that the heavenly doctrine it contains, and the great moral
it reads to us all, may be written in
living

living characters on your hearts and
my own.

A Sower went forth to sow.

The Character of Jesus Christ, as
our Divine Instructor, is here beautifully represented under the image of
a Sower. How many agreeable and
affecting ideas does this suggest! The
first image it presents to our mind is
that of a laborious and anxious Huſ-
bandman, scattering his seed around
him in every direction. It beautifully
intimates to us, that this heavenly
Sower dispenses the good seed of the
word of God with a liberal and un-
distinguishing hand. It is indiscri-
minately thrown upon every human
heart, high and low, rich and poor,
good and bad—it is freely lavished
upon all, without exception—and it
is fruitful or unfruitful, according to
the quality of the soil that receives

B 5   it.

it. The feed this great Sower fcatters upon the world, is as munificently imparted to every rational creature, as the common light of the fun, and the common blefling of air and water. For God and Chrift, who have opened, for the benefit of the world, thefe inexhauftible treafures, would have all men to be faved, and to come to the knowledge of the truth. It is not the fault of the Sower, when this feed is blafted, and fails of arriving at its defigned maturity. This is entirely owing to the badnefs of the foil to which it is committed, and to the bad difpofitions, depraved affections, and corrupted and corrupting paffions that are fuffered to blow, and blaft, and kill it. The nature and quality of the feed difperfed by this great Sower upon all hearts, good and bad, without diftinction, is originally and uniformly the fame—of the fame intrinfic excellence and

and essential goodness—the fertility, or infertility, is entirely owing to the principles which are in that heart that receives it. If its principles and dispositions are bad, they choak the good seed of the word of God, and render it unfruitful. If the heart is bad, it loses all its moral principles of vegetation—it has neither the love of God to warm and foster it, nor the love of virtue to animate and quicken it. Upon such an heart the dews of heaven distil in vain—the showers of heavenly grace and truth spend their virtue ineffectually—it has no principles in it to animate this seed, or that in the least conspire to carry it to its maturity. The seed therefore, that is graciously sown by an almighty hand, perishes, finding nothing to fructify and fertilize it. It is sown in vain upon such a bad heart, where either the flames of lust scorch and shrivel it, or the floods of intemperance drench

drench and drown it. The feed which Jefus fows into the human heart will not ftrike root, and fhoot forth in all its native lovelinefs and beauty, unlefs it have the funfhine of the divine life to enliven and invigorate it, and the gentle gales of meeknefs, mildnefs, and love, to fan, agitate, and mature it. Think how odious in the fight of God that heart muft be, that receives the good feed of the word from the impartial hand of our Redeemer, but difappoints all the hopes of the great Hufbandman. Think how deteftable in the fight of the great Searcher of our hearts that mind muft be, whofe adamantine hardnefs neither the fhowers of heaven can foften, nor all the beams of divine grace and love form and mellow into fertility and ufefulnefs. How beautiful are the words of the Apoftle upon this head—his language is highly figurative, and truly inftructive and

fublime.

sublime. *The earth*, says he, *which drinketh in the rain, which often falls upon it, and bringeth forth herbage fit for those for whose use it is cultivated, receiveth blessing from God; but that which beareth thorns and thistles is rejected, and nigh unto cursing, whose end is to be burned.* Both the good and the bad heart equally receiveth, you see, the friendly rain of heaven, *that often comes upon it.* That often comes upon it—in what form and mode doth it often come—in sermons, in prayers, in public worship, in reading the Scriptures and good books, in returning Sabbaths, and all the various means we all enjoy for religious instruction. What could the blessed God have done more for his vineyard, than he hath done! He hath sent his prophets, one after another, to dress and cultivate this vineyard—he, at last, caused the Sun of Righteousness to rise upon it, with healing under

his

his wings, to difpel the noxious mifts
in which it was enveloped, to chafe
away every thing unpropitious to its
cultivation and utility, and is now de-
puting his minifters, the fellow-la-
bourers of Chrift and his Apoftles, to
drefs and till it, and render it a delectable fcene of diftinguifhed beauty
and happinefs. God hath done every
thing, confiftently with his perfections, and the freedom and liberty of
the human will, to render the good
feed, which he hath fown, a vital
principle, productive of the fruits of
holinefs and happinefs. If we fuffer
this principle to be choaked in fecular purfuits, to be corroded away by
avarice, to be drowned in intemperance, to be entombed in felfifhnefs,
to perifh through floth, and idlenefs,
and negligence, and thus render it unfruitful, God is clear—the blame is
ours—God implanted this heavenly
feed in our hearts, to be the principle of
our

our higheft felicity for both worlds—
it was we who killed it by our lufts,
fuffered it to languifh and die through
our fatal inattention, and voluntarily
forbore to heap around it thofe good
affections and difpofitions, which, under the bleffing of God, would have
caufed it to take root, and fpring up
to life everlafting.

Moreover, it is to be obferved, that
the *field*, in which this Sower went
forth to fow, is the world.   This is
our Saviour's own interpretation of
this part of the parable. *The field*,
fays he, *is the world*.   The foil, into
which the feed is caft, is the human
heart.   That is a beautiful figurative
defcription which the Apoftle ufes
concerning Chriftians; *Ye are God's
hufbandry*; or, as the Greek word fig-
nifies, Ye are God's *cultivated field*.
The great God hath previoufly prepared your hearts for the reception of
the

the feed he fows—he hath endowed
you with every difpofition and affection proper for enlivening and per-
fecting that divine principle, which
was intended to conftitute your happinefs, and, both by reafon and revelation, hath put your minds in the
beft ftate for producing a copious
harveft of eternal happinefs.   Let me
then ferioufly put the queftion to you;
Will you fruftrate the defign of God
in carrying you to the perfection and
happinefs of your natures ? Are you,
can you be fo loft to all fenfe of your
welfare and intereft, as to fuffer all
the culture of the bleffed God, all the
indefatigable pains of the divine
Jefus, all the unwearied labour of
the holy Apoftles, all the means the
Gofpel employs for the improvement
and eternal happinefs of your immortal fouls, to be loft upon you ? Hath
the breaft of any of my audience contracted fuch an hardnefs as to be un-
fufcep-

susceptible of all impression—so callous by impenitence and a course of wickedness, as that even the Word of God is sown in vain, is incapable of striking root, is blasted, sickens, languishes, dies, for want of what—, Why only of goodness of heart to cherish and inform it with life. Depraved creature! how wickedly dost thou counteract the goodness of thy God, and defeat the compassion of thy Redeemer, art the executioner of thine own happiness, I might say, by shutting thy heart against the reception of that seed which the hand of God profusely scatters—suffering it to die floating upon the surface, for every airy pleasure to pick it up, and for every ravenous lust to devour it, and all thy happiness with it. Let me ask thee, Will God forgive thee for letting thy heart, which he hath stocked with such an amiable variety of the noblest and best

prin-

principles, grow, through thine own wilful neglect, into a fteril, dreary, inhofpitable, ufelefs wafte? Doft thou convert the paradife of God into a wildernefs, and fuffer the ample field of thy heart, which God defigned fhould be embellifhed with an amiable variety of ufeful virtues, to be overgrown and choaked with noxious and baleful weeds.   O what an enormous perverfion is this of the goodnefs of God—what an ignominious degradation of our natures—what infamous floth, not to ftrike a fingle ftroke to eradicate a luft, not to have the power to ftrike a fingle ftroke to kill a *root of bitternefs* that begins to fhoot its luxuriant branches, and ingrofs all the virtuous nutriment left in our hearts.   To what bafe and abject impotence does floth and idlenefs reduce a man, that a rational being can fee ruin before him without exerting a fingle effort to efcape it? Do you ever think

what

what confufion will cover you, if it be found at laft, that you have fitten fo many years under the Gofpel and are altogether unfruitful—that the good feed of God's holy Word was indeed fown into your hearts, time after time, fabbath after fabbath, but it would never fo much as ftrike root—for what reafon—it could never fo much as ftrike root in a heart that was nothing but one wild region of fantaftic pleafures, fenfual defires, and fordid fecular principles.

God is infinitely merciful. He watcheth with great patience over impenitent obdurate finners. It is with great reluctance he gives them up to an impenetrable hardnefs of heart. *He fpeaks to them once, yea, twice,* but man regardeth him not. It is a tender affecting defcription, and fhould have all its weight with us, where the bleffed God is reprefented as coming

year

year after year, reasonably expecting
fruit when so much had been done
for his vineyard, but finding none.
But think of those aweful words, God
grant they may never be fulfilled in
any of you : *Cut it down immediately :
why cumbereth it the ground any longer ?*
One would really think that common
ingenuity, that common gratitude,
would make men tear from their
hearts every principle inconsistent with
their obligations to God and Christ,
the best and greatest of all benefac-
tors. One would think that a sense
of duty, a sense of interest, would
induce men to bring their hearts under the influence of these saving truths,
and carry an irresistible force with
them, to prevent them from frustrat-
ing the gracious designs of God, and
losing an immortal soul——for ever wilfully losing an immortal soul. But
those, alas! who are determined to slight
the Gospel, to slight their ministers, to
slight

flight good books, to flight the fabbath, will never be convinced of the
worth of the foul, the value of the
Gofpel, and the neceffity of holinefs——
I mean, will never be convinced in
this world——the punifhments which
God will inflict in another world will
fully convince them of the worth
of thefe things. Let us enter upon
every new week, month, and year,
with folemn refolutions, avowed in
the prefence of God, that we will improve our time better, that we will fuffer the good feed of the word of God
to take deeper root in our fouls, that
we will cultivate our powers with
greater affiduity than we have yet done,
fpend our fleeting moments to better
purpofes, take more pains to improve
ourfelves in knowledge and holinefs, and, by our induftry, with the
bleffing of God, gain a greater meet-
nefs and preparednefs for an eternal
world.

I   Per-

Permit me to make another general remark upon this parable, before I defcend in fome following Difcourfes to difcufs the particulars of it. One cannot but obferve how beautifully the nature and progrefs of religion in the foul are reprefented by feed fown in the ground. Religion, grace, the principle of holinefs, the divine life, call it by what names you will, is fmall in its beginning—when it is depofited in the genial foil of the human heart, it ftrikes deep root—it receives increafing vigour from the good difpofitions in which it is implanted—it grows up and flourifhes in all its native beauty—it diffufes fhowers of fragrance round the whole ample extent of all the foul's capacities—and, when arrived at its maturity, is a great, and glorious, and divine fpectacle, which God, Chrift, and angels, view with a peculiar fatisfaction. *The kingdom of God is like a grain of muf-*
tard-

tard-feed, which a man took and fowed in his field. Which indeed is the leaft of all feeds: but when it is grown, it is the greateft among herbs, and becometh a tree: fo that the birds of the air come and lodge in the branches thereof. We fee the nobleft of the works of men rife to the greateft grandeur from fmall beginnings—empires, commonwealths, cities, a contem, ole handful of men—nothing but an obfcure town or village, at firft, perhaps—yet in length of time, by a feries of fuccefs, by the dint of induftry, and a continual indefatigable attention to the arts of peace and war and commerce, have at laft attained to an immenfe glory, and to the higheft pinnacle of terreftrial greatnefs. So it is with the divine life in the foul of man. At firft the principle of it is weak and inconfiderable—by culture and improvement it gains greater and ftill greater ftrength—the dews of
heaven,

heaven, the grace of God, co-operate with human endeavours to promote and forward its growth——'till at laſt it breaks forth in all its immenſe lovelineſs, in all its rich variety of divine beauty, and gladdens the eye of every ſpectator. *So is the kingdom of God,* ſays our Lord——the *kingdom of God,* that is, religion in the ſoul——*is as if a man ſhould caſt ſeed into the ground, and ſhould ſleep, and riſe night and day, and the ſeed ſhould ſpring and grow up, he knoweth not how. For the earth bringeth forth fruit of itſelf, firſt the blade, then the ear, after that the full corn in the ear.* Mark how gradual the progreſs of the divine life is—— firſt the ſeed ſown——then the blade—— next the ear——and at laſt full corn in the ear. From this progreſſive nature of perſonal religion it is, that we are ſo frequently exhorted to *grow in grace,* to *add to our faith virtue,* not to be continually laying the firſt

prin-

principles of the doctrine of Jesus, but to go on to perfection. _

APPLICATION.

This is a subject which greatly concerns us all——the declension or the progress of Religion in our souls. Let us then solemnly put the question to our own hearts——Is the good seed of the Word of God, which the great Sower hath freely scattered over my heart, a vital principle? Have I suffered it to fix deep root and flourish in my soul, or suffered it to languish and die? Do I suffer piety to God to animate and quicken this seed, and holy and virtuous dispositions to promote the great principles of its vegetation?——or do I permit every airy pleasure to pick it up, and every secular pursuit to choak and kill it? Do I ever gratefully acknowledge the merciful hand that dispensed this good seed——or have I duly prepared

C   pared

pared my heart for the reception of it?
Do I find it fpringing up in my foul to
everlafting life——or is its growth and
progrefs checked and ftopped by the
baleful weeds I have fuffered to take
deep root in my mind, and intercept
its nutriment? Let me earneftly im-
plore every one of you carefully to
examine the ftate of his mind, and
impartially afk his confcience——Confcience will faithfully tell——whether he
is gradually going on towards perfection, or gradually relapfing into a
cold inactivity and carelefs indiffe-
rence. Lord, by thy bleffed Spirit
quicken our induftry in the divine
life, and excite every one of us, by
the fedulous cultivation of our minds,
to be continually making a happy
progrefs towards perfection; that the
good feed, which by thy bleffed Son
thou haft fown in our hearts, may receive its full and final completion in
a glorious harveft of immortal bleffednefs!

S E R-

SERMON II.

MATTH. XIII. 4.

And as he he sowed, some seeds fell by way-side, and the fowls came and devoured them.

IN the former discourse I shewed the wisdom of our Saviour in preferring this method of instruction before every other, and represented the many happy effects with which it would be accompanied. I shewed you that by the Sower who went forth

to

to fow, our Lord intended himfelf—
that the field, into which this good
feed is promifcuoufly thrown, is the
human heart—and that this good feed
of the Word of God flourifhes or
languifhes, lives or dies, according to
the goodnefs or badnefs of the moral
foil to which it is committed. I reprefented to you alfo, how happily and
beautifully the principle of the divine
life in the foul is adumbrated by feed
fown in the ground—fmall in its beginning, but, by the dint of conftant
culture and improvement, and the
well-difciplined affections of the human heart, attains its deftined glory
and greatnefs, fills the whole ample extent of the foul with facred and divine
fragrance, and affords a moft delightful fpectacle both to angels and men.
Having made thefe preliminary obfer-
vations, which I thought requifite and
neceffary, as a proper introduction to
this moft beautiful and inftructive parable,

rable, I now proceed to discuss the
several particulars of it. God grant
that the important truths it conveys,
and the lessons of useful instruction it
reads us all, may leave indelible impressions on our hearts!

*A Sower went forth to sow: and as
he sowed, some seeds fell by the way-
side, and the fowls of heaven came and
devoured them.* Our Lord here fitly
represents a heart rendered obdurate
and callous with sensual pleasures, by
a hard beaten path, which nothing can
penetrate. The word of God, which
hath been liberally thrown upon such
a mind, lies naked and exposed upon
its surface, incapable of entering, and
unable to exert its active vital principles and genial qualities. It lies upon
the beaten surface, a prey to every
roving passion, to be picked up and
devoured by every wandering lust. For
by the fowls of the air, which, col-

C 3

lected

lected in large companies, and, urged by insatiable hunger, light upon it, and, with ravenous eagerness, instantly devoured it up, are meant the airy pleasures, the fantastic follies, and the ever-craving, unsatisfied appetites of men, which, if permitted to rage and act the vulture, quickly devour every thing that is excellent, amiable, and virtuous in the mind. All good instructions, all useful admonitions, all the salutary calls to repentance, all the cogent persuasives to a good life, all the friendly advice of parents and ministers, all the tremendous denunciations of Almighty God—all these heavenly feeds are sown ineffectually—rebound from its hard, impenetrable surface—lie useless upon it, without being able to infix the least impression. The heavenly feed, which the gracious Redeemer dispenses, is not able to strike root in a soil so unsusceptible of all moral life and vegetation, impregnated

nated with fo many noxious principles, the bane of every thing excellent and good——a thoufand lufts ftarve it in its birth, prevent and check its growth, or fwallow it up the moment it is fown. It is impoffible that vital Religion, the principle of the divine life in the foul, can grow and flourifh, and attain its proper maturity, when it is implanted in a heart where fo many fenfual paffions are permitted to rife in all their baneful greatnefs, to throw their luxuriant branches around, and caufe every feed, which a divine hand can plant, to languifh, wither, and die. Serious fermons, pious inftructions, virtuous admonitions, lofe all power to affect and imprefs. They fall in all their heavenly mildnefs and felecteft influence, upon fuch an hardened mind, upon a mind fo hacknied in the corrupt ways of men——they fall, but leave no trace behind. What impreffions can be made on a foul that

C 4

breathes

breathes nothing but pleaſure, ſenſual
fantaſtic pleaſure.   What impreſſions
can be fixed on a covetous, ſordid,
ſelfiſh, groveling heart, that is incruſt-
ed with a ſurface hard and impenetrable as adamant !   What impreſſions
can the love of God, and holineſs, and
heaven, make on a mind that is one
univerſal region, inhabited by no better ſpirits than the fiends of ſenſuality,
luxury, diſſoluteneſs, and debauchery,
with the great Demon of luſt preſiding
over them, ſaying to one, Go, and he
goeth, and to another, Do this, and he
doeth it !   What impreſſions can holineſs and goodneſs ſeal upon a ſoul,
that ſeems to live for no end but the
gratification of its worſt paſſions——
which knows, and which is determined
to know, no pleaſure, but what levels
it with the brutes——I ſhould rather ſay,
degrades it infinitely below the brutes !
What impreſſions can be made on a
ſoul, whoſe waking and whoſe ſleeping
hours,

hours are employed in fondly contemplating the glare and glitter of pomp and fplendour——who knows no pleafure, no happinefs of life, but while it treads a giddy round of trifling amufements, is ideally for ever prefent in foft, delufive, idle fcenes, that diffipate every thing ferious and virtuous, and running an eternal circle of the moft abandoned gratifications that the moft abandoned of mankind ever invented ! Can the heavenly feed, which God, and Chrift, and weeping parents, and faithful minifters fow, find a reception in that bofom that is *hardened by the deceitfulnefs of fin*——poffeffed with a fatal perfuafion that fuch and fuch a purfuit is the only road that leads to true happinefs——ridiculing every argument, and every perfon, that *fternly pronounce the rigid interdiction*——and deliberately refolved to regard nothing that would four and leaven their miferable joys, or debar and avert them from their

C 5

grove-

groveling and wretched indulgences. Virtuous inftruction, affectionately thrown upon fuch a mind, is beautifully defcribed by our bleffed Saviour, as good feed, caft upon a hard beaten path—incapable of penetrating it—lying naked and ufelefs upon it—the food of every devouring paffion—the prey of every infatiable defire. With all the celeftial qualities with which it is endowed, it is unable to impregnate fuch a worthlefs foil with any moral fertility—its furface, beaten by the light fantaftic foot of fuch an infinite tribe of gay, airy pleafures, for ever prevents its reception—its growth is precluded—it finds nothing in a region, trampled by fuch a vain and vifionary group, to enliven it, and unfold its vegetating principles—and the good Being, who fowed it, with forrow and regret fees it picked up by every unclean bird, and gradually devoured by every ominous and ill-boding fowl.

1   More-

Moreover, the feed, that fell by the way-fide, which the fowls of heaven · inftantly devoured, beautifully reprefents thofe who hear the word of God with negligence and carelefsnefs, with no previous well-formed difpofitions at all to receive inftruction and improvement from it. By this part of the Parable thofe are aptly defcribed, who attend public worfhip without bringing, or defigning to bring, its facred transactions to their immortal fouls, or thinking themfelves at all interefted in its great concerns. Alas! what unhappy numbers are there of this unhappy clafs of hearers! How many are there, who regard the fabbath rather as a wife political eftablifhment, as a happy political relaxation from the drudgery of life, than as a divine inftitution appointed by our Maker to preferve through all ages of the world, in the minds of his creatures, a fenfe of their dependence,

ence, and of the worth of their immortal fouls. How many are there, who feem to think that Religion is rather the bufinefs of a particular fet of men, than the great concern of all men. In the prefent age Public Worfhip feems to be looked upon as a fort of Theological Entertainment, that agreeably or difagreeably returns once in feven days, to chequer and diverfify the dull fcene of life—and people attend upon this fingular amufement with pretty much the fame difpofitions as they do upon other amufements—to make their remarks upon the delivery of the public fpeaker,— upon the propriety or impropriety of his ftyle—upon the elegance or inelegance of his manner—upon the juftnefs or unjuftnefs of his fentiments— forgetting all the while that they have either minds to be improved, or fouls to be faved. How juftly is the moral ftate of thefe perfons characterized by the

the *seed falling on the beaten path, and the fowls of the air devouring it*— who enter the doors of a Christian Church from no other motive, with no other view, but an idle principle of curiosity——to exercise their critical penetration——to applaud or condemn the language, the diction, the elocution, the opinions of the preacher—— eagerly catching every thing that will feed this most unseasonable and criminal vanity——suffering their passions to be titillated and inflamed, but their reason and understanding to remain unenlightened, unimproved——not once regarding how seriously, and holily, and devoutly the worship of God is conducted, but only how elegantly, and pleasingly, and charmingly it is performed. The Scriptures well describe this idle and worthless disposition, by *itching ears,* that pay more regard to sound than sense——whose vanity and false taste is soothed and gratified

tified by flowers of rhetoric, a gaudy
pomp of ftyle, and the empty jingle
of fuperficial declamation.   No wonder, if the good feed of the Word of
God remains unfruitful, for it cannot
penetrate a mind, whofe furface is
only affected by the impulfe of empty
found and light fantaftic ornament
and decoration—entirely regardlefs of
the native worth and divine excellence
of the feed that is fown—folely attending to the *manner* in which it is
fown.   Such difpofitions are not fitted
to retain good inftruction—it is totally
loft upon fuch a vitiated tafte—a depraved imagination, a falfe erroneous
judgment, prevent it from entering
into the intimate effence of the foul—
the heavenly truths, which are dif-
penfed by the preacher to render immortal fouls wife and happy, lie naked and ufelefs upon the fteril uncultivated furface, and a troop of airy
fantaftic paffions, imagination, fancy,

cy, tafte, fafhion, with their light
pinions defcend upon it, and inftan-
taneoufly pick it up.

The fame deplorable effect, rendering the Word of God unfruitful,
arifes from another unhappy caufe——
when men enter a worfhipping affembly with their hearts full of religious
controverfy——full of fpeculative fyftem
and fentiment——environed by prejudice——held faft in the adamantine
fetters of bigotry and party-fpirit——
difpofed not fo much to receive edification and improvement, to have
good principles fixed in their minds,
to have their hearts inflamed with the
love of God and their Redeemer, as to
judge of the foundnefs or unfoundnefs
of the preacher's Creed. I do not
know a more wretched abufe of the
worfhip of God than this——perfons
coming into a Chriftian congregation
of worfhippers with no other view than

to

to pick up phrafes—to treafure up in their memories fuch and fuch obnoxious expreffions—not once confidering how many ferious and practical things were faid—forgetting thofe truths in which all men are agreed; and confequently all men moft concerned—intending to forget them—but hoarding up in the mean, narrow, gloomy cell of a controverfial fpirit every thing fpoken that does not exactly fuit with their particular opinions. How much hath practical religion fuffered by controverfy, by the miferable Shibboleth of a party fpirit ! How vainly, how ineffectually, is the good feed of God's Word fown upon an heart, full of religious difcord, and religious controverfy ! What a fhameful, what an impious perverfion of Chriftian Worfhip, to bring with us into the houfe of God our irritable paffions, a litigious, captious fpirit, lying at catch for words and

expref-

expreffions, when our hearts and thoughts ought to be employed on far different fubjects than thefe! What an infult is fuch a temper as this to the bleffed God, who prefides in eve-ry religious affembly, and who fees and knows from what principles our devotions flow. Are our fond prepof-feffions, our doubtful opinions, our miferable controverfies about particu-lar points of no confequence to the caufe of vital Religion, an acceptable facrifice, think you, to God—or is fuch an inflammable fpirit in a proper ftate for approaching the facred pre-fence of a pure and holy Being. Thefe things are the bane of true Piety—thefe unhappy prejudices with voracious greedinefs light upon every thing that is ferious and devotional, and devour every thing they find in the heart, that is holy, heavenly, and good. —

With

With these very dispositions the Jews in our Saviour's time attended his public ministry. They came with all their Jewish prejudices and Rabbinical notions about them. They heard his heavenly doctrines with minds inveloped in all the darkness of system, and with understandings fettered in the strongest chains that superstition ever forged. What was the consequence, and what will ever be the consequence of persons hearing the Word of God with such unhallowed dispositions as these? Did they receive any benefit even from the personal instruction of the Son of God? Were they affected by the *gracious words that proceeded from his mouth?* Could the blessed Jesus, with all his heavenly mildness, grace, and love, soften their obduracy, overcome their prejudices, and subdue their system? O the force of prejudice! O the invincible power of long-conti-

continued habits—of a long-continued
superstition! Even the beloved Son of
God, who spake as man never spake,
who wrought such miracles as mere
man never wrought, and published
such discoveries as no human teacher
ever before delivered, could not, you
see, impress the hard obdurate heart
of a Jew—could not convince him of
the folly and falshood of his system—
could not dissolve those chains which
riveted his heart to his beloved Rab-
bies and his beloved Temple, and
bring him to the acknowledgment
and conviction of the truth and divinity of his mission and doctrines.
Hear our blessed Lord's complaint:
The heart of this people is waxed gross,
quite callous, quite unsusceptible of
all impressions; *their ears are dull of
hearing, their eyes they have closed, left
they should be converted, and I should
heal them.* Alas! this hath ever been
the case in all the ages of the Christian

tian Church. The very same cause hath rendered, and, I am afraid, will ever render, in a great measure, the Word of God unfruitful. How can the grace of God, the principle of the divine life, strike its roots in a mind that pays a greater regard to *words* than things——that has only a form of Godliness, but is a stranger to the power of it——that considers Religion rather as an art or science, full of technical words and learned phrases, which he must learn——and is more solicitous to fill his head with notions, than his heart with holiness. Can any thing correspond more exactly to the *seed that fell by the way-side*, on an hard beaten, unimpressible path, an easy delicious morsel to the greedy hungry fowls, than the unhappy mind of that Christian, who reads and hears, and worships, and yet suffers his prejudices to stop all the avenues that lead to his heart? How can the

fair

fair harveft of holinefs, the glorious harveft of eternal life, fpring from a foil that is poifoned by party-fpirit, and totally contaminated with the itch of controverfy? When the heavenly feed falls upon fuch a hard and beaten highway, as fuch an heart is, a thoufand paffing and repaffing prejudices trample it under foot, fully and ruin its celeftial beauty and worth, and immerfe its divine excellence in the fink and filth of the moft abject and ignoble paffions.

Do reflect for one moment, how much the intention of God, in the inftitution of public worfhip, is defeated by our harbouring fuch unworthy principles as thefe. By our unholy difpofitions we convert that into an houfe of contention, which God defigned fhould be the houfe of devotion. By bringing a controverfial fpirit with us to the divine altar, we extintinguiſh thoſe very affections which God intended ſhould be cheriſhed and inflamed. We ſubſtitute theory for practice, form for godlineſs, opinion for piety, and appearance for reality. What God originally intended ſhould inſpire us with ſentiments of love and gratitude to him, ſhould fix in our hearts good principles, ſhould conciliate us to each other, and unite us in the moſt engaging, endearing friendſhip, one to another; we, by a moſt unnatural and impious perverſion, make it a public day of uncharitable diſputation, the Pulpit is unworthily converted into a ſtage of railing and invective, and immortal ſouls reſort to our worſhipping aſſemblies, not ſo much for improvement in holineſs, as for improvement in the arts of religious altercation. Thus it is that the good ſeed of the word of God periſhes through the badneſs of the ſoil to which it is committed. Thus it is

that

that we abuse and defeat the gracious
designs of Almighty God in appoint-
ing the Sabbath, in continuing a Gospel ministry, and putting into our
hands the sacred Volume, by voluntarily turning our mercies into mise-
ries, and our liberty into licentiouf-
ness. Thus it is that we pervert the
grace and goodness of God and Christ,
by suffering every vain pleasure to devour the good principles they have
sown in our hearts, by allowing our
lusts, and appetites, and bad habits,
first to starve, at length to kill it, and,
by our own folly and madness, most
wretchedly suffering that to wither and·
die, which, by timely prudence, care,
and improvement, might have been
reared into a goodly plant, and blessed
us with the immortal fruit of eternal
life.

APPLI-

APPLICATION.

I shall close this Discourse with the following Reflections.

Let none of us frequent the worship of God as a matter of mere form and custom, and discharge it in a careless, negligent, and perfunctory manner. Many people attend public worship because it is the custom of the country in which they live—or the fashion of the place in which they reside. But I must recall these words—alas! In the present age it is neither customary nor fashionable to attend divine worship. Men seem to think as if they could be saved as well without it, and live as if that great Being, who hath solemnly said, *Remember the Sabbath-day, to keep it holy,* would never call them to account for their wilful violation of it. The command

mand to keep holy the Sabbath-day was the very firſt command that God enjoined upon man. Let us ever reverence this *firſt and great commandment.* Let us count our Sabbaths a delight, make conſcience of attending public worſhip, and attend with a Chriſtian temper, with a holy and devout diſpoſition. Let us on this day be open to conviction, never bring our worſt paſſions with us, rankling in our breaſts, to the Divine Preſence: but let our ſpirits be calm, our minds compoſed, and all our affections and powers in a fit diſpoſition for receiving inſtruction and edification. *Take heed how you hear,* ſays our Lord. And we read of perſons, whom the word of God did not profit—why—what prevented—becauſe it was not mixed with faith in them who heard it. O Sirs, better we had never entered the doors of a worſhipping aſſembly, if it do not find us more holy, and charita-

D   ble,

ble, and leave us fo. *Keep thy foot when thou goeft to the houfe of God, and be more ready to hear, than to give the facrifice of fools.* To the fame purpofe the Apoftle : *Therefore we ought to give the more earneft heed to the things that we have heard, left at any time we fhould let them flip.* For a creature to ftand in the prefence of its Maker, praying to him, hearing his word, and chanting his praifes, is a folemn tranfaction. Let not our hearts be endowed with fuch principles, and hardened with fuch depraved difpofitions, as that this good feed of God's word, which Minifters difpenfe, falls upon it, but is not able to penetrate its furface, and the dews of heaven, the grace of God, and the influences of his Spirit, diftil upon it, but cannot foften its obduracy, cannot feal any impreffion upon it. It is a beautiful defcription of a devout and holy hearer of God's word, which the A-

poſtle James gives us.——May its importance ſtrike and affect us all——*Be
ye doers of the word, and not bearers
only, deceiving your own ſouls. For if
any be a bearer of the word, and not a
doer, he is like unto a man beholding
his natural face in a glaſs: for he be-
holdeth himſelf, and goeth his way, and
ſtraightway forgetteth what manner of
man he was. But whoſo looketh into the
perfect law of liberty, and continueth
therein, he being not a forgetful bearer,
but a faithful doer of God's word, this
man ſhall be bleſſed in his deed.*

D 2

SER-

SERMON III.

MATTH. xiii. 5, 6.

Some fell upon stony places, where they had not much earth; and forthwith they sprang up, because they had no deepness of earth: and when the sun was up, they were scorched, and because they had not root, they withered away.

THE Parable of the Sower is intended to represent the different dispositions of those who hear the word of God. Its variety of success in the

D 3

world.

world, the different fate it meets, according to the good or bad state of the heart that receives it, is beautifully described in apt and striking images. This is a subject in which we are all intimately concerned. A faithful picture of the heart of every Christian is here portrayed, and held up to his serious and impartial contemplation. Every one, who now hears me, falls under the denomination of one or other of these different hearers, who are in this moral picture so accurately delineated.

Our Divine Master had a perfect knowledge of the human heart. He knew all the passions by which it was agitated——all the principles by which it was governed——all the various affections and dispositions by which it was actuated. He had an infallible discernment of the spirits of men, and knew how persons of such and such affections and habits would act in such and

and such circumstances. He was acquainted with the moral state of every person with whom he conversed—was conscious of the motions of his mind, the principles of his actions, and the temper and frame of soul with which he attended. Thus St. John observes, that our blessed Saviour *needed not that any should testify of man*, that is, that should give him an attestation of any man's character, for *he knew what was in man*, he had a perfect, distinct, and infallible knowledge of the hearts of men. This appears from the whole of his History. How often does this expression occur in the four Evangelists, *Jesus knowing their thoughts!* How often does he discover to his Disciples things which they had studiously concealed from him, and openly show them the folly and unreasonableness of designs, and schemes, and deliberations, which they had privately agitated among themselves, and

to

to which they never imagined he could be witness! And how stupendously does this divine knowledge of Christ appear, in the most accurate and exact descriptions of the various tempers and dispositions of mankind! How very differently different men stand affected towards the word of God, and what different effects divine and heavenly things have on different dispositions, is most beautifully and instructively shown in the various Parables he rehearsed. If we attend to these Parables, we shall discover in them a knowledge of mankind that was more than human. They are faithful pictures of life, in which all the various features of the human heart, so to speak, are minutely traced out, and exhibited in the most striking light.

In the Parable we are now considering, our Saviour, in the most apt and
expressive

expreffive images, reprefents how differently men are affected by the word
of God, and the reafons which pre-
clude or promote the moral fertility of
the divine life. He holds up this faithful picture to our eyes, that we may
judge for ourfelves, how far fuch and
fuch a particular figure in it reprefents
our own ftate, and is a copy of that
original we carry in our own hearts.
By thefe faithful reprefentations he
leads us to judge by comparifon—
that is—to pafs a true verdict upon
the ftate of our own fouls, when compared with fuch and fuch a character
as drawn by him, and puts the queftion
to our own heart: How far do I re-
femble this defcription—in what rank
of thefe different hearers does my confcience clafs me—is my heart like the
beaten path on which the word of God
is able to make no impreffion—or is
it like the ftony ground, covered
with a flight and fcanty foil, into which

the

the word of God falls indeed, but is
not capable of arriving at its maturity, by reason of the impenetrable flint
that lurks beneath——Or is my heart
one universal wild and wildernefs, in
which the heavenly feed, fown from
time to time upon it, is ftarved and
choaked by the luxuriant weeds of fecular care, fordid covetoufnefs, and
earth-born paffions, which I have fuffered for a feries of years to flourifh
there without controul, and to canker
and kill every good feed which a divine hand hath planted.   Thefe, or
fuch as thefe, are obvious reflections,
which the various characters, drawn
in this Parable, fuggefts.   And this is
the very ufe our Lord intended we
fhould make of it —— to compare
our hearts with his defcription——to
bring our affections and fpirits to that
ftandard of holinefs and goodnefs he
hath laid down——to examine our hearts
by thefe rules, and impartially judge
how

how far we conform to or deviate from them——to be often viewing our minds in that faithful mirrour he holds up to us, to rectify what is amiss, and cherish and improve what is holy and good. May God of his infinite mercy grant that this may be the practical instruction which the heavenly doctrine of our blessed Redeemer may teach us all——and may the Spirit of God indelibly engrave these important and saving lessons on the fleshly tablet of our hearts.

The seed which fell upon stony places, slightly covered with mould, is a just and affecting representation of the generality of Christians. What numbers of men, who attend public worship, and read religious books, are here described! At the time they are hearing or reading, they are greatly affected, greatly impressed——but no sooner do they mix in the active scenes of of life, but all these slight impressions are totally obliterated. At the time they are hearing a Discourse upon such a subject, or reading a good book upon such and such Duties, their convictions are awakened, they see in the clearest, strongest light, the reasonableness and importance of such and such a course of life, and breathe some faint wishes, utter some ineffectual sighs, express, it may be, some momentary resolves, that they will follow such useful advice——behave better than they have done——that they will go and sin no more——that they will not be seduced by bad company, in the manner they have been, or, at least, so often as they have been——but will, for the future, direct their steps into such and such a path of life, which the Preacher, or the Writer, so faithfully tells them will lead them to true happiness. By the arguments addressed to them they are convinced, fully convinced,

that

that the courfe they are purfuing is a ruinous and deftructive one to their healths, their conftitutions, and to their immortal fouls——For a fhort interval, a fhort tranfient gleam, they have a ftrong, full view of thefe momentous concerns——perhaps for a time they abhor and deteft themfelves for the exceffes and enormities they have foolifhly incurred——they fee, they manifeftly fee where thefe courfes will end——and for a few hours or days are greatly ftricken, deeply penetrated with a fenfe of their condition. One would think, from fuch a warm and genial reception as this, which they give to the feed of God's word, that it would indeed not be fown in vain, but would bring forth its fruit in due feafon. One would conclude, but, alas, it would be a too hafty, a too precipitate conclufion, that the word of God, which falls into a foil fo foft and fo fufceptible, that generoufly, as one

one would think, opens all its powers
to receive it, would find nutriment
enough, would ftrike its roots, fpring
up, and blefs us with the immortal
fruits of true repentance and holinefs——But alas! all thefe convictions
are temporary——they laft no longer
than the Sermon——it is well if they
laft as long as the Sabbath. Thefe
painful convictions of mind, thefe
awakened terrors of confcience, are
indeed, as the prophet beautifully de-
fcribes them, but *like the morning cloud,
or the early dew, that foon paffeth away.*
The Word of God is affectionately dif-
penfed by Minifters——the grace of God
falls upon fuch an heart in fertilizing
fhowers; but our preaching is vain,
and the grace of God is repulfed, and
falls in vain. The heart indeed with
gladnefs receives it——fondly opens its
bofom to receive it——it finks into it——
but cannot fink deep, for the adamantine rock that is but juft, juft beneath.

neath its furface. The center of fuch
an heart is one entire mafs of hard impenetrable rock, which defeats all the
moral principles of vegetation that
there may be in the flight furface
with which it is furrounded. For
when the love of pleafure is enthroned
in the heart——hath erected its palace
in the very center of its dominions,
and fways its abfolute, uncontroulable
fceptre——what power can a few tranfient good difpofitions have to fubvert
a monarchy that hath been fo ftrongly
eftablifhed——what power can a few
momentary virtuous affections have,
which only hover round the bounda-
ries of this empire, to weaken its
foundation, and to demolifh this im-
pregnable fortrefs! Perhaps, thefe
very people, who are fo affected with
a particular Sermon, on fuch a particular fubject, that for a time comes
home to their bofoms and confciences,
would be as much affected by a ten-

der

der pathetic scene in a tragedy. And there is but too great a resemblance betwixt the effects that follow the one and the other. A few tributary tears flow, perhaps we do not know well from what cause they flow—purely from mechanism—we are in both instances hurried away by our passions, while our understanding and reason remain unenlightened, unconvinced, not once consulted. How is it possible but convictions must be fugacious, ineffectual things, when they flow from passion, not from reason. What lasting saving impressions can be made on a mind which is hardened by sensuality, and its whole internal substance petrified into stone, by a life of unfeeling debauchery and voluptuousness — Such worthless creatures may be impressed by an affecting Sermon, or a good Book, just as they are impressed by reading an interesting Novel, or the idle soothing pages of an Eaſtern tale.   But mark the conſequence, the never-failing conſequence——The Church is no ſooner diſmiſſed, or the book laid aſide, but the moment that pleaſure invites, the moment that ſcenes of amuſement call them, that the mercenary harlot ſpreads her net, and the importunity of company begins its ſoft compulſion, but theſe abject, miſerable ſlaves follow——all impreſſions are in a moment effaced——and the fair harveſt of reformation and amendment, which their late convictions pleaſingly gave us to hope——which ſprang up ſo inſtantaneouſly, and indeed ſo unexpectedly——is in one fatal moment ſcorched——its riſing beauty all ſhrivelled up——in one and the ſame hour, it may be, it bleſſes us with a thouſand opening beauties, but is immediately killed, and dies——and we turn our eyes from it as a loathſome, worthleſs ſpectacle.

Oh

O with what pleasure do some people attend Public Worship—almost with as much pleasure as they go to hear some celebrated actor, who hath the entire command of all their passions. O what satisfaction do some people express on hearing such a Preacher—almost the same satisfaction as they receive upon hearing a new Performer, who never trod the stage before——With what delight will they expatiate upon the propriety of his manner——the justness of his sentiments——the sublimity of his subject——the perspicuity of his reasoning——and the importance of the truths he delivered. They sit impressed and affected——they go away serious and thoughtful——But the moment the sun of pleasure arises upon them——the moment the great never-setting Luminary of nocturnal and diurnal pleasure throws his dazzling infatuating beams around them——it is scorched——and because

their

their light shallow minds did not afford it deepnefs of earth, it withers away.

It is not hearing many Sermons, or reading many books, that makes men religious and wife—but reflecting on what we hear and read. Repeatedly hearing great numbers of folid well-compofed difcourfes, and perufing great numbers of inftructive and useful books, is in itfelf of no more value, than any other amufement we might happen to be fond of—unlefs we revolve and meditate what we hear and read—convert theory into practice—make our improvements in virtue correfpond to our improvements in knowledge—and caufe the progreffive acquifitions of erudition and literature, we from time to time attain, to fhine forth in a worthy, ufeful, unexceptionable converfation. Books hold up to us a faithful glafs, in which we

may

may fee, from a vaft variety of examples, what we are to avoid, and what
purfue.   Sermons contain many an affectionate perfuafive to our duty and
happinefs, many an affectionate dif-
fuafive from fin and mifery—It is the
ufe we make of thefe that determines
our characters—that determines our
wifdom or our folly. If we forget
the ufeful truths we read, if we flight
the falutary admonitions we hear, the
fault is not in the Preacher or Writer—
they have delivered their fouls—the defect is merely in our own hearts—
there the obftruction lies—there is
the rock from which divine inftruction rebounds. and which defeats all
the culture that heaven beftows.   It
is to little purpofe that we were furnifhed with the faculties of underftanding, the powers of improvement, and the means of holinefs, if
we do not bring with us previous
good difpofitions for making that facred

cred and virtuous use of them our
Creator intended we should make.

Our Saviour, in very lively images, sets before us the conduct of
such persons, on whose soft ductile
minds impressions are soon made, and
soon effaced. *When the sun was up,
they were scorched; and because they
had not root, they withered away.* The
seed sown in the thin mold, that
environed the internal mass of stone,
appeared in a fair and flourishing
state, till the hot beams of persecution assailed it—then, *for want of
moisture,* meaning for want of integrity and principle — it instantly
shrank and shriveled, faded and
died. What a true representation is
this of great numbers of professors!
What warm, zealous advocates are
they for the interests of Religion,
while they can but enjoy it unmo-
lested!

lefted!—but the moment it is ftricken
at by the fecular arm, they abandon
and abjure it, and do not think the pro-
feffion of it of fuch moment, as will
juftify their facrificing their temporal
intereft for the fake of it. In the funfhine of national profperity how fondly and indolently do men recline under the fhade of their religious principles!—but let the ftorms of perfecution arife—let but the ax of the
bigot be laid at the root of the tree,
under which they foftly repofe, and
they fhake with unmanly terrors,
bafely renounce the caufe they had
efpoufed, and turn apoftates with the
utmoft facility and unconcernednefs.
Let but their principles be in
danger, and they publickly difavow
them. They deem it their duty to
follow Chrift, but will not take up
their crofs to follow him. They are
pleafed with religious liberty, and the
full poffeffion of the rights of confcience—

science —— but if a sudden torrent should overwhelm these, they fail supinely down its stream, without exerting a single effort to check and stem it. In times of liberty and tranquillity they are all zeal and oftentation——in times of diftress and perfecution they relapfe into the meaneft pufillanimity, and the moft bafe and abject cowardice.

Hear our Lord's explication of this part of the Parable. *He that received the feed into ftony places, the fame is he that beareth the Word, and anon with joy receiveth it; yet hath he not root in himfelf, but dureth for a while: for when tribulation or perfecution arifeth becaufe of the Word, by and by he is offended.* O how odious in the fight of God and Chrift and angels and good men, is fuch a mean-fpirited, cowardly, daftardly foul——that would facrifice confcience
a nd

and integrity to any man or body of
men, who fhould defire and purchafe
fuch a facrifice—that would make
fhipwreck of its faith and its religion,
rather than rifk any part of its worldly
intereft in the facred caufe. What
muft the great Searcher of our hearts
think of our principles, when he
knows we will adhere to them fo long,
and no longer—while we enjoy the
quiet, undifturbed fruition of them.
How muft we appear in the eyes of
the great Spectator, when we make
ufe of our Religion, juft as an exte-
rior badge, to put on and put off, juft
as will beft fuit particular times, and
particular feafons—to be any thing
and nothing, according to the hu-
mours of thofe with whom we con-
verfe—and according to the emergencies that arife—and to give into
every mean and bafe compliance, rather than in the leaft endanger our dear
perfons, and our dearer fortunes. Can
any

any thing be a greater proftitution of the facred caufe of religion, than to abjure and abandon it, whenever it comes in competition with our fuppofed reputation, and our fecular interefts. *He that loveth father and mother better than me, is not worthy of me,* and he, who in fuch conjunctures, when his religion is ftricken at by fanguinary zeal, bigotted fuperftition, and erroneous principles——he who in fuch conjunctures *doth not take up his crofs, and follow* his Redeemer, is not worthy to be called his Difciple.

That is a very inftructive Parable which our Lord addreffes to us, the great moral of which is, That before we engage in religion we *fhould fit down and count the coft*——impartially examine our hearts, whether we fhall be equal to the difficulties to which we may be expofed for the fake of it——and whether we fhall renounce.

E

nounce it, or fupport it, if God fhould call us to fuch a conflict.

It is well known with what undaunted refolution the primitive Chriftians fupported the heavieft perfecutions, and endured the moft cruel tortures. They went with a ferene countenance, with a noble heaven-infpired intrepidity, to the ftake, to the racks and wheels of their heathen perfecutors—and thofe of them, few and inconfiderable indeed, who made a public recantation of their Chriftianity, rather than fuffer for it—who, when the *fun* of perfecution rofe upon them, *were fcorched,* and *for want of moifture withered and died* — thefe were ever treated by the whole body of Chriftians as the moft infamous and abandoned wretches — were univerfally fhunned by them, and never admitted into the pale and communion of the Church.

4   The

The cafe is juſt the fame with regard to any religious principles, of whoſe truth we have the firmeſt perſuaſion, and fulleſt conviction. If we ſurrender up theſe, whenever they are attacked—if we deſert thoſe principles which our conſciences and our Bibles tell us are true, whenever ſecular emoluments happen to interfere with the profeſſion of them—if we refuſe to countenance and ſupport thoſe Miniſters whom we know preach the truth as it is in Jeſus, and forſake thoſe Churches which are formed upon the baſis of religious liberty, and the rights of conſcience and private judgment, and are guilty of theſe mean and miſerable compliances, rather than be gloriouſly ſingular in oppoſing the general torrent of corrupt principles, and riſk any thing, though it be in the cauſe of the unalienable rights and liberties of mankind—if this be our abject ſpirit, the repreſenta-

E 2   tion

tion of our Lord in the text suits us
as exactly as if we had sat for the picture. *When the sun is up*, when persecution lights her fire, or lifts her
ax, all our former principles are instantly no more.

APPLICATION.

Of what infinite concernment is it
to every one of us, that our hearts be
right with God. Think what integrity, what religious integrity is, and
how useless and contemptible every
thing is without it. Our religion is
good for nothing if it will not bear the
test of persecution. It is a mere name,
a mere external thing, a splendid outward badge, that has no connection
with our hearts; it is a painted mask,
which we assume or drop as best suits
the times. If our religion have not penetrated to the center of our hearts,
have not occupied and possessed the
whole

whole heart, it will be better for us to lay the profession of it all aside. What good will it do us to *have a form of godliness, and know nothing of the power of it?* If the internal mass of our hearts be nothing but one entire adamantine rock of impenetrable flint, what service will it be to us to have a thin flight surface of mould around it, in which nothing that is sown can ever come to any maturity? *Be not deceived, God is not mocked. Whatsoever a man soweth, that shall he also reap.* The harvest in the other world shall be according to the goodness or badness of every man's heart into which the seed is now sown. *He that soweth to the flesh shall of the flesh reap corruption; but he that soweth to the Spirit shall of the Spirit reap life everlasting.*

E 3

SER-

SERMON IV.

MATTH. XIII. 7.

And some fell among thorns: and the thorns sprang up and choaked them.

OUR Saviour having, by various images, reprefented the reafons which prevent or retard the rife and progrefs of Religion in the fouls of men, comes now to mention, among the principal caufes which obftruct its growth, a worldly covetous difpo-

E 4 fition.

sition.   In his explanation of the Parable of the Sower to his Disciples afterwards, he thus expounds the meta-
phorical expressions I have now read
to you.   *He that received seed among
the thorns, is he that heareth the Word;
but the cares of this world and the deceit-
fulness of riches choak the Word, and
he becometh unfruitful.*

In discoursing, therefore, on these
words, I will illustrate the beautiful
similitude here employed by our Saviour, will represent to you the truth
of his observation, and show how incompatible such a mind, as is here
described, is, with all the principles of
moral culture and religious improvement. · May God grant, that what at
this time shall be delivered on this
important subject may be useful in
rectifying the disorders of our minds,
in expelling every thing from our spirits that is narrow and contracted, and
engaging

engaging us to contemplate and to pursue the riches of eternity.

Before I enter upon the direct discussion of the doctrine of my text, suffer me to premise this observation. It was never the design of our Saviour and his Apostles to represent riches as abstractedly evil, and to condemn the acquisition of them. It is true, we meet with many passages in the sacred Writings, where the very phrases rich and wealthy are used as terms of the same import with profligate and abandoned, and the very expression, riches, is synonymous with wickedness and guilt. Our Saviour declares it to be as morally impossible for a rich man to enter into the kingdom of heaven, that is, to become a professor of the Gospel, to embrace a Religion that was despised and outraged, as it would be for a cable, as some understand the passage, to be thrust through the eye

E 5 of

of a needle.   By the rich in this paffage, as he afterwards explains himfelf to his Difciples, who were alarmed
at this harfh expreffion, he meant thofe
who trufted in their riches, made them
their great idol, the fole object of
their worfhip, and pronounced nothing
great and good and happy, but what
was fplendid, oftentatious, and magnificent.   And in many other parts
of Scripture, when we repeatedly
read fuch paffages as thefe : *How
hardly fhall thofe who have riches enter
into the kingdom of God—Go to now,
ye rich men, weep and howl for the miferies that are coming upon you—Not
many great, not many rich, not many
noble, are called*—we are not to under-
ftand thefe paffages in an abfolute,
but a reftrictive fenfe—not as if riches
of themfelves utterly difqualified their
poffeffor for holinefs and heaven, and
the mere poffeffion of them neceffarily
excluded a perfon from all pretenfions

fions either to prefent virtue or future
happinefs.   For it is not the ufe but
the *abufe* which the Scripture con-
demns.   It is not fuperior wealth and
opulence,   but the bad difpofitions
they too commonly produce, which
the Scripture notes with marks of in-
famy.   So far is the Scripture from
prohibiting the acquifition of wealth,
that it excites men, of all profeffions,
by every incentive and argument, to
a laudable induftry, to be diligent in
their refpective ftations, to adorn them
by frugality, œconomy, and activi-
ty—the only road this, the only happy and worthy arts thefe to riches and
honour.   So far is the Scripture from
reprefenting riches as fimply and abf-
tractedly evil and unlawful, and neceffarily productive of temporal wickednefs
and everlafting perdition, that it reprefents them as the diftinguifhed
bleffings of Almighty God.   It promifes them as rewards, does not de-
nounce

nounce them as punifhments. It
teaches us to regard them as bleffings,
which the Providence of God annexes
to our fobriety, induftry, and frugality—as fignal benefactions, fhowered
down upon us by his munificent hand
—and as temporal retributions, divinely conferred upon us, to crown
our active virtue, and reward our honeft labours. Superior riches are fuperior bleffings, beftowed by Providence as fuch—they are the means,
the intended means of enjoying fuperior happinefs—and there is not a
happier being on the globe than a rich
man with benevolent difpofitions.

If we pervert this kind and merciful donation of God to us, we counteract the defign of the donor—it is
a moft ungrateful, a moft unnatural
perverfion—and it is not the fault of
the giver, but of the receiver, if we
convert thofe things into curfes which
he

he intended to be blessings. Riches are most to be envied, as they enable their possessor to do so much good— to dissipate so much distress as there is in this world—to do so many friendly beneficent offices as the various occurrences and emergences of this life give him an opportunity of performing—I mean—of cloathing the naked, feeding the hungry, encouraging merit, and softening the various rigours of human wretchedness. If happiness is entirely a mental thing, can there be a nobler, purer, sublimer happiness enjoyed on this side Heaven, than what arises from the heart-felt consciousness of our having relieved a real object of compassion, or our having made a poor, indigent, numerous family a scene of joy and gratitude?- No pleasure on earth like this. No happiness on earth can be compared to the happiness of doing good. And are we not, ought we not to be infinitely indebted to the

2. pro-

providence of God for enabling us, by bleffing our induftry, and grant-ing us a happy feries of profperity and fuccefs, to enjoy this diftinguifhed fe-licity ? *Does not every good gift, and every perfeEt gift, defcend from the fa-ther of mercies ?* And does not this fig-nal bleffing among others, which ena-bles us to do fo much good, and to enjoy fo much happinefs from the con-fcioufnefs of having done it ? So that the obfervation of an ill-natured Di-vine hath more impiety and wit than truth and juftnefs in it, who has this remark : " One may plainly fee from " this," fays he, " that the Almighty " accounts riches to be worthlefs things " from the worthlefs charaƐters on " which he beftows them."

It is not opulence and wealth, which, abftraƐtedly confidered, are eminent bleffings and fuperior privileges ; but the wretched abufe and the finifter mifim-

mifimprovement of them, which produce the fatal effects here mentioned
by our Saviour.   It is not gold, but
the luſt of gold, which *chokes the Word
of God, and renders it unfruitful.*   Of
all vices, avarice renders the human
heart the moſt unfuſceptible of good
impreſſions.   A mind inflamed with
other deſires is, comparatively, tender and impreſſible — but a ſoul
centered in ſelfiſhneſs is abſolutely
incorrigible.   Beſides, a taſte for ſenſual exceſſes laſts not always — the
paſſions and purſuits of youth are re-
dreſſed and rectified by the ſolid reflections and deliberate judgment of
manhood — or, at leaſt, ſometimes
accompany us no farther than the cool
and ſober evening of life—but cove-
touſneſs, when once it hath infuſed
its poiſon in the heart, is ſeldom or
never expelled—it gains freſh ſtrength
in every ſtage of life through which
we paſs, and in our ſad frail decline,
                                    when

when every other paffion hath left us,
this ftill, ftill binds our hearts to dirt
and pelf in adamantine indiffoluble
fetters.   One of the ancient Philofophers fomewhere fays, That the love
of fame is the laft garment a good
man lays afide—I think it is equally
true, that the love of money is the
very laft paffion of which old age di-
vefts itfelf.   Yet perhaps there is not
a more ridiculous abfurd farce acted
on the ftage of human life, than extreme avarice in extreme old age. To
be grafping at a perifhing world, that
we muft foon clofe our eyes upon for
ever—to be cherifhing boundlefs defires of hoarding and accumulating,
while bowing under all the infirmities
of frail mortality—to be fpending
anxious days and nights in planning
projects, concerting meafures, and
weaving elaborate fchemes to amafs
wealth, to dupe the incautious, to purchafe fuch an eftate, to make up fuch
                                 a fum,

a-fum, when the fhades of a long evening are ftretching over us—what con-
fummate folly and diftraction is this!
How muft Angels pity and defpife
us! pity our wretchednefs, and defpife our prepofterous folly, to fee a
dying creature, juft going to bid an
eternal adieu to the world, clinging to
it as if it were to fpend an eternity in
it? What muft the bleffed God and
fuperior Spirits think of our conduct,
to fee us, when juft tottering over the
brink of life, extending our hopes
for many, many happy years yet to
come—travelling in idea to fuch and
fuch a *city, and continuing there a year,
to buy and fell, and get gain*—exulting
perhaps over the ruin of our fellow-
creatures—to fee others fo poor and
fo fallen, while we are fo rich and fo
raifed—and what is the moft ridiculous circumftance of avarice in old
age, worthy the derifion of all mankind, is, amidft all the vaft treafures
they

they have accumulated, to be haunt-
ed with the moſt dreadful apprehen-
ſion, that they ſhall die for want of
common neceſſaries !

Any paſſion whatever, that is ex-
ceſſive, hath reduced, and does and
will reduce men to phrenzy and di-
ſtraction—but ſooneſt of all will the
inordinate, inſatiable love of the
world do this. For young people to
ſtudy and exerciſe the art of frugality, parſimony, and œconomy, I had
almoſt ſaid for young people to be
covetous, is comparatively commend-
able, laudable, and virtuous. They
have many revolutions and viciſſi-
tudes in life to encounter—many un-
expected, unforeſeen emergencies with
which to ſtruggle—and many ſad re-
verſes, it may be, to experience—
but for old age, which hath now paſſed
the troubled ocean of life, and is juſt
within ſight of ſhore, inſtead of ſa-
luting

luting the wished-for port, instead of entering it with shouts of triumph, and sequestering themselves in a calm and peaceful retreat——to put out again upon its dirty and dangerous waves, still to struggle with its storms and tempests, and never cease plowing its billows, and roaming for the wealth that lies beyond them——never cease, even *when our body and strength is consumed*, conflicting with its winds and surges, till they fatally wreck us, and ingulph us in their bosom——Oh what delusion and madness is this! Well might our blessed Lord, in his explanation of this part of the parable, style it, the *deceitfulness of riches.* For what a series of egregious deceit do they practise upon us——luring us on insensibly, insensibly from one stage of life to another——duping, and for ever ruining us at last——by the glitter of this vain tinsel dazzling the eye of the soul, and preventing it from seeing the

the only true riches, the riches of eternity.

What miserable slaves, and abject despicable vassals, does this DECEIT-FULNESS OF RICHES make of man-kind—in time, perhaps in no great length of time, establishing an empire over their minds, which, as long as they live, they never have the power to dissolve—holding the understanding, and reason, and conscience, in eternal chains, and letting loose all the mean and mercenary passions to tyrannize without controul. *Love not the world*, says St. John, *neither the things that are in the world. If any man love the world, the love of the Father is not in him. Ye cannot*, says our Lord, *love God and Mammon.* One passion must predominate. The heart cannot equally be governed by two opposite principles—and where the

the love of money governs, it will take care to admit no competitor.

What an ignominious, what a deplorable degradation is this of an immortal soul! How is the glorious sun, which God lighted up in the soul, eclipsed, totally obscured and shrouded by these baleful shades! *If the light, that was in thee,* is thus darkened by this groveling earth-born passion, *how great is that darkness!* How can it be expected that the heavenly seed, which the hand of God sows upon such a heart, full of such sordid passions, should be able to strike root, and to come to any degree of beauty and maturity! How can it otherwise happen, but that when it falls, as frequently it does, in Sabbaths and Sermons and convictions, into a soil overgrown with such poisonous weeds, it must instantly be lost and choked among them,

them, and die, for ever die, for want
of the leaft good affections, the leaft
warmth of benevolence to revive, and
fofter it ! How can the good feed of
the Word of God exert its divine
principles, fpring up in celeftial beauty, and diffufe around a fhower of
heavenly fragrance, when fo many
noxious thorns and luxuriant weeds
overtop it, weave their thick peftilent
branches over it, excluding the funfhine of divine grace, and hindering
the dews of heaven, the genuine influences of the Bleffed Spirit from falling upon it, and infpiring it with life
and vigour !

The principles in the heart of a
worldling are infinitely incompatible
with the divine life. The love of
God is a noble and generous paffion :
the love of the world a narrow, illiberal, and groveling one. The grand
governing principle in a true Chriftian's

tian's heart is universal charity : the sole animating principle in a worldling's soul is a boundless rapacity. Religion is founded on the love of God and man : worldly-mindedness is founded on a base and miserable self-love.

Nothing can be more diametrically repugnant to the life and spirit of Religion than the canker of self-interest. An avaricious selfish temper is totally opposite to that generous and beneficent spirit the Gospel breathes. How infinitely abhorrent are the principles that lurk in a miser's heart from the genius of a Religion whose distinguishing crown and glory is benevolence ! What pretensions can he have to the character of a Christian, who is yet to feel the power of charity ? There is something in earthly-mindedness that is peculiarly subversive of the great end and design of the Gospel,

pel, and, of consequence, infinitely destructive to our everlasting interests. Well might our Lord observe, who had so infallible a knowledge of the human heart, that the seed of God's Word falling upon a spirit, overgrown with such sordid principles, *would be choked*, be instantly suffocated and overwhelmed by their uncontroulable predominance. For it is impossible that holiness and heaven should find any seat in a heart that is one vast gloomy dome sacred to Mammon.

To prevent this sordid and ignoble passion from gaining an ascendency over us, let us frequently attend to those pathetic dissuasives which the Scriptures are continually sounding in our ears. God Almighty is also every day solemnly admonishing us against contracting and cherishing these earth-born passions. The language

guage addreſſed to us by every death we behold, by every funeral we attend, is this —— *Set your affections on things above, not on things on the earth: Lay up for yourſelves treaſures in heaven,* which are liable to no accidents and caſualties, which Time and Death will never wreſt from you. The conſtant mutability and tranſiency of life, the uncertainty and inſtability of human condition are perpetually warning us of the folly of idolizing the world, rivetting our ſouls and affections to objects that muſt be very ſoon torn from us, and which will be of no avail to us either on a ſick bed, and in the hour of death, or conſtitute any part of the happineſs of that eternal world into which we are juſt removing.

How many pathetic and inſtructive leſſons does our Redeemer affectionately read us, who was deputed by

F   Al-

SERMON IV.

Almighty God from Heaven to fhew us the true path of happinefs, and to f.ve our fouls. His precepts, his example, his doctrines, promifes, and difcoveries, the whole fyftem of his religion is calculated to extinguifh in our breafts a paffion for the world, to difengage our affections from fugitive and tranfitory objects, and to turn the eye of the foul ftrongly and intenfely upon the great and glorious realities of Eternity. One would think, if any thing would make us tear the world from our fond embrace, and repulfe it from us with Chriftian difdain, it would be the hopes, and views, and profpects of our bleffed religion——One would think, if any thing would prevent us from degrading and debafing our original from God, from difgracing and difhonouring our glorious redemption by Chrift, and infpire us with a dignity and elevation of foul, worthy our Maker, worthy

worthy our Redeemer, and worthy that immortality after which we are taught to aspire, it would be that assurance of an endless futurity, which God, by Christ, hath implanted so deeply and indelibly in the human heart. But if men will sell their Christian birth-right for the most frivolous and paltry considerations—if men will part with the things that are not seen, only because they are distant and remote, for the things that are seen, and are but temporary—if men will give up all their glorious reversionary hopes in futurity for acquisitions and enjoyments that will very soon leave us, or we leave them, and think themselves abundantly recompensed—if men are determined to act in this foolish wretched manner, they must take the consequences—Nothing will convince them—The voice of the Almighty is uttered in vain—the menaces of Scripture are

F 2 denounced

denounced in vain—the great work of Redemption hath been executed in vain, and through their fecular principles, and abandoned avarice and worldly-mindednefs, they put it out of the ordinary power of God to convert and fave them. The fordid filth and pelf collected about their hearts *choak the good feed, and render it unfruitful.*

With what pathetic vehemence does our Saviour caution his followers against fuch a temper and fpirit as this! How folicitous is he that the minds of Chriftians fhould be confecrated to worthier and fublimer purfuits than thefe! How affectionately doth he diffuade us from harbouring fuch fordid difpofitions! And what cogent and engaging arguments does he addrefs to us, in order to kindle in our breafts a more juftifiable flame. Take no thought, faying, What fhall we eat?

2   What

What shall we drink ? What shall we wear ? How shall we diversify our meals, in order to make a change ? Lay not up for yourselves treasures on Earth, where moth and rust do corrupt, and where thieves break through and steal : but lay up for yourselves treasures in Heaven. Labour not for the meat that perisheth, but for that which endureth to everlasting life. To shew us moreover, by an affecting narrative, how miserably this *deceitfulness of riches* deludes men to their everlasting ruin, by fondly inducing them to make sure of time and a long life, the most fatal of all delusions, he recites for our benefit the following most striking Parable, which, as it is applicable to my present subject, I will now conclude with rehearsing. And he said to them, Take heed, and beware of covetousness ; for a man's life, the happiness of his life, consisteth not in the abundance of the things

which

which he poffeffeth—It HAPPENED that the immenfe eftates of an opulent perfon proved uncommonly fertile, and yielded him an exceedingly rich and plentiful crop—His heart exulted when he viewed the waving golden harveft—and as he looked over the wide-extended profpect, he faid to himfelf—What fhall I do with it all !—Where fhall I depofit it !—I have no place capable of containing half this immenfe crop !—After fome time fpent in anxious deliberations, he cried out in a fudden tranfport—I am determined immediately to pull down my barns—and I will erect grand and magnificent ftorehoufes, where I will amafs all this copious and amazing produce of my fields—When I have piled it all up—I will then fay to my foul—Happy foul ! diftinguifhed is thy felicity ! Thou haft immenfe treafures, from which thou wilt derive fubftantial blifs for a long, long feries

of

of many diftant happy years—come, indulge thy foft envied repofe—feaft on the moft delicious viands—tafte the moft exquifite liquors—and traverfe a circle of every amufement and joy—But while he was brooding over this enchanting profpect, and fondly anticipating all its happinefs—God faid to him, O thou unthinking mortal! this very night the lamp of thy vain life fhall be extinguifhed—and what advantage to thee will then all the immenfe treafures be, which thou haft accumulated!—Like to this vain wealthy fenfualift is every one's end, whofe heart is folely engroffed by riches, and totally alienated from God.

SERMON V.

MATTH. XIII. 8.

But others fell into good ground.

OUR Saviour having specified those moral defects in particular characters, which either totally prevent the reception of Religion, or retard and blast its growth and progress, closes the Parable with describing a good mind, and the fair and copious fruits with which it is adorned. *And others fell into good ground, and*

F 5

brought

brought forth fruit, some an hundred fold, some sixty, some thirty fold. Beautiful and striking is the imagery—truely elegant and happy is our Lord's figurative representation, characterizing a good heart, with all its well-cultivated affections, by a good soil, with all its genial influences.

The similitude is apt and pertinent in several respects. For example—a foil, naturally good, is strongly imbued and impregnated with the principles of vegetation, and answers the wishes of the husbandman who improves and dresses it. In like manner, a good mind is essentially endued and deeply penetrated with the excellence of Religion and moral goodness, and, by the happy improvements it is continually acquiring, accomplishes the ultimate end and design of its Creator—Good ground receives and cherishes in its fertile bosom the good seed which the hand of the husband-

man

man fcatters upon it : a good heart is open to the reception of truth and virtue, and with tranfport receives all thofe communications of light and knowledge, which, in fucceffive periods of the mind, the Providence of God imparts—Ground naturally good, in a happy expofure, mellowed by froft, warmed by fnow, foftened by fertilizing fhowers, faturated with the generous influences of the fun, prepared by culture, and planted with good feed, bleffes the tiller with an ample harveft, bleffes the paffing traveller with infinite delight, when he beholds, in one vaft extenfive profpect, its golden ears, waving upon the ground—bleffes the poor, if free from the curfe and canker of envy, with antedating views of plenty—and bleffeth its proprietor with riches and diftinction. The human foul alfo, naturally good, proceeding pure and unfpotted from the hand of its pure and fpotlefs Former, if preferved from the pollu-

pollution of vice, if carefully guarded
from the defilement of animal paſſions,
and the contagion of bad examples, it
retain in a great degree its priſtine
purity and honour inviolate, and, by
the care of parents, by the good principles inſtilled in education, and its
own convictions of the unrivalled importance of theſe things, it make them
its ſtudy and purſuit, cautiouſly avoiding every thing that would contami-
nate its mind, and deprave its heart,
ſolely intent upon religious and virtuous improvements, tranſported with
a generous inſatiable paſſion for truth
and uſeful knowledge, aſſiduous and
indefatigable in the inveſtigation and
purſuit of every thing that may embel-
liſh and ennoble the human mind; and
in all this courſe of enquiry making
the improvements of the heart keep
pace with the endowments of the
head — a mind that hath been bleſſed with theſe advantages in early life,
that hath preſerved the tablet of its

heart

heart unstained by any great and flagrant crimes, that hath, by the dint of sedulous culture, maintained its animal propensities under proper and virtuous discipline, that cherishes the best dispositions, that has all its powers possessed with the love of God, the love of mankind, the love of truth, the love of virtue, and that makes its supreme happiness consist in that best imitation of God, DOING GOOD—what an amiable spectacle is such a mind, endowed with such principles, both in the sight of God and man! This is the most consummate excellency and highest perfection human nature is capable of attaining. This is that superlatively happy soil which produces the hundred fold, the amplest harvest that the human mind, in this state of imperfection, is enabled to produce.

Vast and almost unlimited are the capacities of the soul. It is impossible

ble to fay what acquifitions in literature cannot be attained. It is amazing
to reflect what improvements in Arts
and Sciences the prefent age hath
made—what difficulties the genius
and induftry of men have furmount-
ed—what infinitely diffimilar and heterogeneous branches of learning!—
for example—a profound fkill in an-
tient languages, and the ftudy of the
moft abftrufe parts of the Mathema-
ticks, have united in one man—and
what immenfe and aftonifhing attainments in Philofophy and Erudition
our intellectual faculties are capable
of accumulating, by the dint of indefatigable diligence, and the habit of
patient and fedulous application! And
the improvements that the human
mind hath made, and is formed capable of making, in religion and virtue,
that nobleft, that divineft fcience, have
been truly confpicuous and illuftrious.
In the lives of eminent perfonages,
whofe virtues hiftory tranfmits to us—

Pro-

Prophets — Apoftles — Confeffors — Philofophers — and Divines — in thefe worthy characters, which fo eminently adorned and dignified our common nature, are held up to us, and to all fucceffive ages, a faithful mirror, which reflects upon us the luftre of their divine and human virtues, and ftrongly reprefents to us thofe vaft attainments in religion and holinefs, of which, by the love and ftudy of heavenly things, our fouls are formed fufceptible. And the hiftory of the lives of thefe great and good men in paft ages and nations, as it affords us the moft rational and ufeful inftruction, fo it fupplies a pleafing entertainment, as it is agreeable to the reflecting reader to fee, in their refpective characters, the happy foil that refpectively produced, fome the thirty, others the fixty, others even the hundred fold, the higheft fummit of human attainment, according to the different abilities and different opportunities with

which

which they were favoured. History, like our Lord's Parables, is moral Philosophy teaching by example. Here we have a faithful exhibition what we are, and what we were designed to be ; what a lovely and amiable thing human nature is, when adorned with religion, when displaying in the brighteft manner that divine image which its good Creator hath impreffed upon it, when carrying its rational and moral powers to the higheft degree of perfection it is qualified to reach, and when afpiring after every religious attainment and mental endowment that may exalt and adorn its nature, and accomplifh the wife and gracious intention of God, in furnifhing it with thefe enlarged capacities, for making thefe fignal improvements, and enjoying this diftinguifhed felicity.

In difcourfing on this part of the Parable of the Sower I fhall confider what conftitutes the worthy and excellent

cellent character here represented —
Some fell into good ground.

Goodneſs of heart comprizes the
whole circle of the virtues. When
we ſay, A perſon has a good heart,
the idea conveyed is, that ſuch an
heart is a beautiful epitome of every thing that is amiable and laudable among men. It denotes probity, ſincerity, honeſty, integrity, benevolence, candour, piety, friendſhip, every generous and lovely quality. By the *ſeed* therefore *which fell
among good ground* are ſignified thoſe
who are poſſeſſed with the principles
of religion and virtue—who have do-
cil, ingenuous, and well-diſpoſed
minds—whoſe actions and conduct
flow from conſcious integrity and inward goodneſs—who ſtudy to ſecure
the approbation of their own hearts,
rather than the applauſe of the world
—whoſe ambition it is to *be,* rather
than

than to *seem* good—and who cherish the best affections both towards God and man.

The love of God is a principal ingredient in this universal character. Indeed there cannot be any thing great and distinguished in a character that is not formed upon the love and imitation of God. A principle of piety has the strongest influence in framing and disciplining the human heart. *The fear of God is the beginning of wisdom,* and a reverence of the Deity, when habitually infixed in the soul, is the most powerful incentive to invigorate and establish the active and social virtues. He, who hath accustomed himself to contemplate the transcendently amiable character of the Divinity, with devout joy and sacred rapture dwells on that inexhaustible benevolence, that infinite compassion, that omnipotent power, that unerring wisdom, and that

that boundless goodness which constitute the endearing character of the
Being we call God, cannot but feel
his heart irresistibly attracted towards him——cannot but love a Being,
in whom all these excellencies unite,
with all the powers and affections of
his mind——cannot but be powerfully
induced to practise those duties which
will recommend him to the favour and
acceptance of such a Being——and be
engaged to imitate the Deity in those
moral perfections which constitute the
dignity and lustre of his character, and
which solely constitute the excellence
and worth of the rational character.
To form that virtuous and worthy
character here represented, it will be
useful to consider the approbation of
the Deity as the greatest felicity and
blessing we can enjoy, and to reflect,
that the Being, who now is perfectly
acquainted with our sincerity and integrity, will one day most certainly re-

ward

ward it. He who by habitual reflection makes the thought of God's
presence with him, wherever he is,
familiar to him, cannot but have a
good heart—for piety is the mistress
of the virtues—they shine with inferior radiance around her, as the lesser
constellations around the fair Regent
of the night—Piety, devotion, and
the reverence of God, are the noblest
source of moral, practical virtue—
have the greatest efficacy in harmonizing all the affections and dispositions of the soul, and inspiring them
with their proper animation and vigour.

Representing to our minds, therefore, by serious contemplation, the
presence of the great God as an ap-
proving Spectator of our sincerity and
goodness—thinking how such kind affections, such benevolent desires, such
a course of action, must recommend
                                        us

us to the friendſhip and complacential love of the bleſſed GOD, is an argument the moſt forcible and cogent of all others to make us in reality to be what GOD deſigned us to be, and is pleaſed to ſee us be, and to keep our hearts in that frame and ſtate which we *know* that GOD approves, and *feel* that conſcience applauds. Hence it was that the judicious Ancients impreſſed the tender minds of their children with the greateſt reverence of GOD, and inſtilled into them, with the firſt dawn of reaſon, the moſt venerable ideas of the Divinity——wiſely judging that the fear of God is the moſt prevalent and powerful principle that can be fixed in the human heart, and that the veneration of the Deity was the ſtrongeſt foundation on which they could rear the fair ſtructure of every perſonal, domeſtic, and ſocial virtue—— and it will be found that the greateſt Characters that ever appeared in the

Heathen

Heathen world, were not lefs diftinguifhed for their devout adoration and
reverence of the immortal gods, than
they are fignalized for their political
abilities, their mental endowments,
and their heroic atchievements.

I need not mention, in order to
form the good man, what laudable
care Jewifh parents employed to poffefs the minds of their children with
the moft venerable ideas of the great
God—efteeming this the moft compendious and efficacious rule they
could give them to form their morals, and influence the heart—What
pains alfo the primitive Chriftians
took to make their offspring wife,
good, and happy, by imprefling the
foft, fufceptible mind with the moft
reverential conceptions of the adorable
Majefty of God, appears from the
whole hiftory of thofe times—and that
the numbers of men in the prefent
time

time are fo comparatively few and inconfiderable, who pay a regard to principle and confcience, and think integrity, and virtue, and honour fomething
too good to be facrificed to worldly
confiderations, may perhaps in a great
meafure be attributed to the flight regard they were in early life taught to
pay to the Deity——to the levity with
which they were allowed to ufe his
Name——and to the little concern thofe
about them difcovered to make them
think and fpeak of God with any awe
or reverence at all. Take away the fear
of God from the heart, and you take
away along with it all the other virtues.
If the root of this moft vigorous and
all-animating principle be once fub-
verted, all the branches immediately
fade and die. Of fuch powerful energy and divine efficacy is the principle
of religious Piety, and the reverence
of God, to influence the human heart,
to regulate and direct its affections,
and

and eftablifh the foundation of all moral goodnefs and excellence.

But not Piety to God only, but all the moral and focial virtues, confpire to form the character here denoted. It is not enough that fome certain felect virtues, congenial, as it were, to our particular caft of mind, predominate in the heart; but all the human virtues fhould form a brilliant affembly there——humanity, benevolence, meeknefs, humility, integrity, and every moral endowment that can conftitute a worthy and virtuous character.

Amidft this fair train of virtues, Benevolence fhould fhine with diftinguifhed luftre. There cannot be a good heart without it. A mind, that is adorned with every mental and moral accomplifhment, but is deftitute of Benevolence, is ufelefs to the world, and dark as Erebus. *If I give*

give my body to be burned, and all my goods to feed the poor, and have not a real vital principle of Benevolence and Charity actuating me, I am nothing. *Faith, hope, and charity: these three,* says the Apostle ; *but the greatest of these is charity.——In nothing,* says CICERO, *do men approach nearer to the immortal Gods, than in doing good.* Benevolence, flowing from an imitation of God and love of mankind, is the highest perfection of the human character——it is the diftinguifhing glory of the Gofpel——it is the diftinguifhing glory of the Chriftian. If I could fpeak with the tongues of angels and men, and could accumulate all the knowledge and erudition comprized in the whole circle of arts, fciences, and literature, and with all thefe fplendid, oftentatious accomplifhments, have not charity——benevolence of foul, and goodnefs of heart——I am of no more value in the fight of God than founding brafs, or a tinkling cymbal. Su-

G   perior

perior knowledge and superior abilities, when united with the amiable
qualities of the mind, and illustrated
with distinguished goodness of heart,
form a truly useful, venerable, and
conspicuous character——but separate
from goodness of heart, they are dangerous, and the deserved objects of
universal contempt.

This goodness of heart is what
our Saviour in the first place enjoins
his followers to acquire and cultivate. *First make the tree good,* and
the *fruit* will of consequence be
good, and partake of the genial nature
of the tree that produces it. The
heart is the great source of action——
if it be pure, the inferior affections
will be pure. *From the abundance of
the heart the mouth speaketh.* A man's
language takes a tincture from the
heart that prompts it. If the heart be
chaste and virtuous, the conversation
will

will be decent and worthy—if the *in-ward* difpofitions and affections be formed into virtue, the *outward* expreffion of them will be an amiable fanctity of manners. Hence our Saviour's infallible criterion—from the refpective nature of mens actions and conduct, to judge of the true nature of the primary fource from which they flow. *By their fruits you may* infallibly *know them.* A good tree bringeth forth good, a bad tree, bad fruit.

Simplicity and godly fincerity are the moft fhining parts of any character. *Behold an Ifraelite indeed, in whom there is no guile,* was the amiable character of Nathanael, given him by a Perfon who perfectly knew the human heart, and all the virtues which adorned it. And why was this recorded, but to excite us to attain the fame probity and candour of mind, to urge us, by this worthy ex-

G 2   ample,

ample, to acquire true sincerity and genuine goodness of mind, and to let us see how integrity, and virtuous simplicity of manners, will entitle us to the applause and eulogy of the holy and divine Jesus.

What the *good ground* in the Parable here means, and what those fruits are with which it is adorned and crowned, you may see in the following faithful and minute representation. *The fruit of the spirit*, or of a good mind, *is love, joy, peace, long-suffering, kindness, goodness, fidelity, meekness, continence.* Here you have, in delectable prospect, the fair ample region of the human heart, embellished with every moral grace and beauty that can charm our mind, and attract our love.

By the *good ground* is meant every one who has his heart formed upon the

the principles of the Gofpel —who
maintains a vital, influencing fenfe
upon his mind of the worth and excellence of religion—who chearfully
conforms to the will of God—who
keeps his fpirit under the moft virtuous difcipline, who by temperance
preferves his intellects found and vigorous—and by the practice of goodnefs keeps his heart awake and fenfible to another's woe—has his paffions
under good government—his reafon
clear and unclouded, his undetftand-
ing alert and active, his judgment
impartial and unbiaffed, and his mind
difciplined to every good word and
work—How lovely that mind, in
which thefe virtues flourifh! How
amiable that character which anfwers
this defcription in the parable, and
whofe ftudy and ambition it is to
implant a good mind with every
Chriftian virtue and amiable quality
that can decorate the fair and fpacious

G 3

field

field of moral life! How worthily is
such an one employed! What a laudable exercise it is, to be assiduously
occupied in pushing our faculties to
their highest pinnacle—in cultivating
those rational powers which God gave
us on purpose that we should cultivate them—in embellishing the heart
with those virtues and principles, with
which it was the original intention of
our Former that we should adorn it—
and in carrying the enlarged faculties
both of the head and of the heart, by
the best improvement of our time
and talents, to the highest degree of
moral and religious perfection that humanity can reach.

Moreover, it is obvious to be re-
marked, that, as ground naturally
good, will not produce any thing
without the labour and culture of the
husbandman; so the soil of the human heart, though naturally good,
will

will yield nothing excellent and useful, if the same care and diligence be not expended upon it. If a soil, composed of the best principles, and endowed with the most generous qualities, be left uncultivated, it will be overgrown with every noxious weed, and the richer it is by nature, if it be neglected, the more it will be choked with tall luxuriant thistles and rampant useless briars——a faithful picture of a mind neglected and uncultivated. Such a mind produces nothing but what is noxious and hurtful——and the better it is by nature, if it be suffered to lie undisciplined and unimproved, it will yield qualities and principles and dispositions, so much the more injurious, baleful, and destructive. No good to be done without pains and labour, either in natural or moral husbandry. ' The immortal Gods,' says one of the ancients, ' give no bles-' sing to mortals without labour. La-

' bour,' continues he, ' is the tax they
' pay for the happinefs they enjoy.'
Let the hufbandman negleét thedrudg-
ery of agriculture for a few months,
and what a wild and wildernefs his
fields appear——Let the fair region of
the human mind remain untaught and
untutored in the gay fpring of life——
let no culture be applied, no feeds of
learning, morality, and religion fown
upon it——and what a dreary folitude,
what a pathlefs, favage defert it be-
comes ! Great induftry is necefſary,
great cultivation is necefſary, before
we reap the rich and copious harveft.
No pro_refs to be made in knowledge
and literature, without induftry. No
reputation and diftinétion to be gained
without fedulous application. Induftry is that powerful agent that fpreads
fertility and plenty around us, which
fo agreeably diverfifies the face of nature——which covers the fields with
verdure, and adorns them with flocks,
                              ——and

—and whofe magic omnipotent hand turns the vaft machine of active and commercial life with all that infinite multiplicity of movements and wheels innumerable.

Upon Religion and Virtue induftry has the fame benign and friendly influence. Great culture is requifite to form the morals, to direct the heart, and regulate the affections. Steady perfevering application is neceffary for quelling unruly paffions, for fuppreffing irregular defires, and maintaining the harmony, liberty, and happinefs of the mind. It is no eafy conqueft to gain the victory over ourfelves, to have our propenfities and appetites in due fubjection, to make reafon rule, and the inferior defires obey—But then fuch a victory is attainable—by virtuous induftry and virtuous refolution it is attainable—and it fhould ftimulate us to attain it, whatever con-

flict

flict and difficulties it may coft us, to reflect, that we fhall enjoy all the happy confequences of fuch a victory, in the undifturbed peace, the unmolefted tranquillity, the unviolable freedom and liberty, and in all the ferene and divine fatisfactions that virtue can yield. The glorious felicity of the *end* fhould reconcile us to the irkfome feverity of the *means*— and the pleafure and happinefs that will finally refult, ought to infpirit us in all difficulties, how rugged and arduous foever, the furmounting of which is indifpenfably neceffary for fecuring the great ultimate object of all our hopes and wifhes. *Make the tree good,* fays our Lord ; and how can we make it *bear fruit to perfection,* unlefs we carefully lop off its luxuriant fhoots, clear it of every thing that would prevent the principles of vegetation, diligently and fkilfully drefs it, throw from time to time ma-

nure

nure about it, and preferve it in a
goodly ftate of health and vigour.——
And how can we maintain the good
foil of the human mind in its original
goodnefs, and conftantly preferve it in
a beautiful and elegant condition, if
we do not induftrioufly reprefs every
noxious paffion that fhoots, if we do
not kill in its firft rife every baneful
weed, before it blow and fcatter its
feed in every direction——and if we do
not by the dint of moral culture and
affiduity eradicate every bitter root of
envy, malice, fenfuality, intemperance, and every other carnal paffion——
Or how can we keep the region of the
human heart in its moral health and
foundnefs, in a beautiful fimplicity
and neatnefs, if we do not ftrengthen
every good difpofition, eftablifh and
confirm every principle of humanity
and benevolence, cherifh every virtuous defire, however weak at firft,
till we mature and perfect it, and,

2   by

by a life of moral induſtry and application, employed in the beſt purſuits, and the nobleſt cauſe, the cauſe of virtue, attain that amiable character here repreſented, and adorn our minds with all thoſe excellent fruits and virtues, which are the glory of our natures, and the diſtinguiſhed luſtre and perfection of the Chriſtian character.

APPLICATION.

To excite you to this, revolve the following Conſiderations.

This is what God requires. He, who formed the human heart with all its noble train of diſpoſitions and affections, requires you to cultivate this good ground he hath committed to your care. *You are God's huſbandry,* or, as the original ſignifies, You are God's cultivated field. It is his deſire fire you should work while it is called to-day, before the night come when no man can work. The materials he hath provided are good: it is your's by culture and improvement to make them what God intended you should make them. The soil he hath formed is rich and generous; it is dependent on you, by moral culture and diligence, to prevent any noxious seeds from being sown there—to prevent the fatal blasts of ungoverned appetite, the poisonous seeds of bad example, and the scorching sun of sensual pleasure from destroying every useful plant there—and to raise a copious harvest of every lovely and useful virtue, to render you amiable both in the sight of God and man.

This culture and preparation of your hearts will also secure to you the favour and acceptance of your Redeemer. Consider with what complacency

cency muſt the holy Jeſus view a good heart! To have a good heart is to have the greateſt bleſſing the Goſpel can now give. To poſſeſs this, is to poſſeſs that for which Chriſt lived and died. This in the ſight of our Redeemer is of ineſtimable price. Holineſs of heart is the perfection of the Goſpel——the beſt imitation of its Great Author——and the only thing that will entitle us to his future approbation. *Well done, thou good and faithful ſervant.*

This is the deſign of Nature, and conſonant to all the powers and principles of human nature. Virtue is the only true happineſs——the ſole proper glory and felicity of a rational creature. When we begin, therefore, to cultivate this in early life, we begin where God and Nature deſigned we ſhould begin. Our noble powers were not formed to lie dormant and uſeleſs——

they

they were made to be improved—and amazing are the attainments at which they are capable of arriving both in literature and in virtue, by means of laborious and perfevering improvement. Let us then be incited to comply with the firft dictates of Nature; and, agreeably to the will of God, the defign of Chriftianity, and the principles of reafon, let us carefully improve and exalt thofe mental and moral powers, which will yield us an ample produce of happinefs in this world, and in the world to come fhine forth in a glorious harveft of immortal unutterable bleffednefs.

S E R.

SERMON VI.

MATTH. xiii. 8.

And others fell into **good ground,** *and brought forth fruit : some a hundred-fold, some sixty-fold, some thirty-fold.*

WHEN our Saviour afterwards explained this part of the Parable, at the requeſt of his Diſciples, he thus deſcribes this happy claſs of hearers : *He, that received ſeed into the good ground, is he that heareth the Word,*

Word, and underſtandeth it ; who alſo beareth fruit. In which interpretation our Lord particularizes three excellent qualities, which diſtinguiſh theſe worthy perſons, and conſtitute their amiable caraĉter.

They *bear the Word of God*—They make conſcience of attending divine Worſhip — regularly frequent religious Ordinances — do not abſent themſelves from public inſtruĉtion, but eſteem it their duty and their privilege to join in the ſocial ſolemnities of public Devotion.—When preſent in a worſhipping aſſembly, they hear the Word of God with devout and well-diſpoſed minds—they ſit as humble, ingenuous, and virtuous diſciples at the feet of their divine Maſter—receive the Doĉtrines of Truth into good minds, and pay a ſerious, impartial, candid attention to the inſtruĉtions that are delivered.

Conſe-

Confequently, he who brings with him to the houfe of God, or to the perufal of the Word of God, fuch docile and amiable difpofitions, carries with him the very beft qualifications for clearly difcovering and *underftanding* its truths. He that received feed into the good ground, is he that heareth the Word of God, and underftandeth it. A virtuous difpofition is beft adapted for the reception of truth—it is a moral difpofition that is congenial to truth—Sacred Truth fmiles with a benign afpect upon fuch an amiable mind, makes it her temple, and fills it with glory. Vice in its nature is repugnant to truth—its native depravity and darknefs cloud the foul, fuffufe the mental eye with the baleful fhades of paffion and prejudice—it naturally fhuns the light of truth—it cannot bear its heavenly beams to dart upon it—it is both averfe to the ftudy and inveftiga-
tion

tion of truth and virtue, and morally incapable of difcovering and underftanding it. The *natural man*, fays the Apoftle, or, as it ought to have been rendered, the *fenfual man*, one who is under the dominion of his worft paffions and lufts, *knoweth not the things of the Spirit of God*—they appear foolifhnefs to fuch an one, who views them through fuch a falfe medium—*and he cannot know them* : his fenfual affections, his debauched imagination, his corrupt depraved heart, totally incapacitate him for the knowledge and perception of truth and virtue—becaufe thefe moral and divine things can only be *fpiritually difcerned*; can only be contemplated, difcerned, and relifhed by a good heart, by a virtuous fpirit, which alone is propitious to fuch facred enquiries.

What

What infuperable power vice and prejudice have to extinguifh the light of reafon, to put out the intellectual eye, and obftruct all the avenues that lead to the mind and heart, appears from that amazing incredulity and obftinacy of the Jews in our Saviour's time, who refifted all the flood of evidence he poured upon them, and remained unconvinced by all the heavenly difcourfes he delivered, and by all the aftonifhing miracles he difplayed. And ever memorable are thofe words of our Saviour—a leffon to all future ages of the invincible malignity of vice and prejudice—*Seeing they fee, but perceive not : hearing they hear, and underftand not. The heart of this people is waxed grofs ; their ears are dull of hearing, and their eyes have they clofed*—meaning—that their inveterate prejudice againft him, and the total depravity of their minds, held all their rational powers in adamantine

tine fetters, and effectually prevented them from either having eyes to fee, ears to hear, or an heart to under-ftand, the nature and moment of truth, virtue, and happinefs. Where-as he, who hath a fincere, honeft, well-difpofed mind, denoted by the *good ground* in the Parable, and brings with him to the contemplation of Na-ture, or to the ftudy of the Scriptures, a paffion for truth, will clearly fee and underftand every thing effential to his happinefs——for his mind is in the hap-pieft ftate poffible for fuch enquiries, and the great and infinite Source of wifdom will illuminate fuch a mind, guide it into all neceffary truth, guard it from every fatal errour, and by the influx of his light and truth irradiate and invigorate all its capacities. *You shall know the truth*, fays our Saviour, *and the truth shall make you free.*

But

But our Saviour, to fhew us that *hearing the Word* of God with good difpofitions, and in confequence of thefe, *underftanding it*, is far from being fufficient to conftitute the Chriftian character, mentions, as the laft indifpenfable quality, in this happy clafs of men, their *bringing forth fruit.* He that received feed into the good ground, is he that *heareth the Word*, and *underftandeth* it, who alfo bringeth forth fruit. Our Saviour fpoke this, and the Evangelifts recorded it, to affure us, that nothing without practice will be of any avail. He, who underftands the Word of God, and perhaps values himfelf upon underftanding it, muft tranfcribe into his own heart and life the great principles and duties it teaches. *Not every one that faith unto me, Lord, Lord, fhall enter into the kingdom of heaven ; but he that doeth the will of my Father, who is in heaven.* If you know

know thefe things, happy are you only
when you do them.   Then, and then
only, is my Father glorified, when
you bring forth much fruit, and upon
this condition only are you intitled to
the genuine character of my true Difciples.   Chriftianity is wholly a practical inftitution.   Its great object is
goodnefs of heart and holinefs of life.
Its aim is not to make men acute me-
taphyficians, or ingenious fpecula-
tifts, to teach men the art of reafoning and the forms of philofophical difputation.   It difclaims the
wifdom of words, the elegance of diction and compofition—and nothing
could be farther from the mind of its
facred Author and the facred Writers,
than to fill mens heads and hearts with
fect and fyftem, and a paffion for con-
teft and altercation.   The great defign of Chriftianity is holinefs of life.
Its precepts, examples, and promifes co-operate only to this one
great

great end—If this be but secured,
the intention of God and Christ and
Apostles then is answered.   To teach
us to deny ungodliness and worldly
lusts, and to live soberly, righteous-
ly, and godlily in the present world—
for this Christ lived, for this Christ
died, for this Apostles wrote and
suffered!   He hath no pretensions
to the Christian character, whose life
is not a daily Commentary upon what
he professes.   The kingdom of God
is not meat and drink, but righteouf-
ness.   The intrinsic goodness of the
fruit is the only test of the true nature
of the tree which bears it.   A holy
conversation is the grand discriminating badge of a Christian.   If a man
leads a profane, covetous, libidinous,
intemperate life, he is a bad man,
and all the showy zealous pretensions
of such an one to Religion are hypocrisy and delusion.   Such a conduct is
an insult upon that sacred Name by
                        H   which

which he is called.   They are the actions that difcover the heart.   This
is a criterion that is infallible.   This
is our Saviour's unerring ftandard, to
whofe certain determination we may
bring our own and others fincerity.
Let no man deceive himfelf; he that
doeth righteoufnefs, then only fulfils
the Chriftian law.   The Gofpel is a
fcheme to promote real vital Religion, to infpire us with the love of
God and the love of men, to excite
us, by the moft cogent and inter-
efting motives, to the confcientious
difcharge of every focial, domeftic,
and perfonal duty, 'to make men
good princes, good magiftrates, good
parents, good children, good huf-
bands, good mafters, good fervants,
good neighbours, good members of
fociety, good and virtuous, fober and
confcientious in every ftation and re-
lation of life, and connects men of all
orders and degrees, the high and low,
                                    the

the noble and ignoble, the illustrious the obscure, every one, who wears the human form, without distinction of persons, to each other in the endearing ties of Christian affection, benevolence, and love.

He therefore, and he only, whoever he be, rich or poor, parent or child, master or servant, who, in the situation in which Providence hath placed him, *bringeth forth the fruits* of holiness, has then the sole proper evidences of a Christian. For alas! what does a mere national nominal profession of the Gospel signify! What will it avail to have had an external form of godliness, but to have been strangers to the inward power of it! If we believe the Gospel is true, we lay ourselves under an indispensable obligation to live as it directs —— And if we believe it to be true, that its doctrines are most sublime, its mo-

rality

rality most pure, its promises most animating, and that it is a system infinitely worthy of God, and perfective of the dignity and happiness of men, yet, notwithstanding this strong conviction, live as if Jesus was an Impostor, his Religion a fable, and futurity a dream, we are self-condemned, and as miserable hypocrites as ever believed one thing and practised another.

Our Religion is from God; let us live as those who are convinced it is. The Gospel is a Revelation from the God of truth, let its blessed fruits adorn our lives. The New Testament is a compleat rule of faith and morals; let its divine principles shine forth in our conversations. Let us be daily improving in every thing that is amiable and excellent, and if any calumnies should be fixed upon any of us by the tongue of malice, let our

lives

lives confute them. The best refutation of any injurious aspersion is such an unexceptionable life as no good person will believe it. A good life, in general, repels the envenomed shafts of detraction; and will sometimes convert the most virulent rancour and acrimony into faint admiration and involuntary applause—This is the Apostle's rule—Having your conversation honest, says he, that he, who is of the contrary party, may be ashamed, having nothing evil to say against you. Oh, what a lovely, amiable, and divine phænomenon does the Gospel exhibit! the fairest transcript and image of the divine, and the highest glory and perfection of the human nature, when its heavenly genius and principles are transubstantiated into the intimate essence of the mind, actuating the heart, harmonizing the soul, transforming and modelling all its affections, and when all

H 3   its

its celestial fruits, in the most copious abundance, shine forth in all their radiance and beauty, to the ineffable delight, satisfaction and utility of all around. *Let your light so shine before men, that they seeing your good works, may glorify your heavenly Father.*

Thus it appears, agreeably to our Saviour's Parable and his explication, that as good ground then only merits that denomination when it bringeth forth, in ample abundance, its proper fruits to their maturity, so does he only fulfill the Christian character, who hath transplanted into his heart the principles the Gospel teaches, and exhibits to his family, and to the world, in his daily life, its fair, resplendent, and useful virtues.

I shall now enquire what induced our Saviour to specify the very different produce which the good ground respec-

respectively yielded.   *Others fell into good ground, and brought forth fruit; some an hundred fold, some sixty, others thirty fold.*

God hath infinitely diversified intellectual life.   Very different are the abilities and capacities with which he hath endowed men.   What an immense disproportion between the mental faculties, and degrees in intellectual discernment and judgment, in various rational and moral agents.   In sagacity, penetration, and intellectual endowments there was a less interval between LOCKE, CLARKE, NEWTON, and the lowest orders of Angelic beings, than between one man and another.   Nature, or rather the God of nature, hath lavished upon one talents and powers, which he hath seen fit to deny to another.   One man seems to inherit, from propitious nature, a more subtil and exquisite texture of

H 4

mind,

'mind, more delicate fenfibilities, more acute difcernment, a more elegant tafte and genius, a finer underftanding, a more tenacious memory, a ftronger, founder judgment, and far more alert and vigorous powers, than what we fee another *born heir to.* The Ancients faid that *Melpomene,* one of the Mufes, fmiled on diftinguifhed genius at its birth, and marked it for her own.

Great, undoubtedly, is the power of education in refining and polifhing the mind, in unfolding and enlarging the mental powers, and giving them a generous advancement and diffufion. But the materials which Nature offers to the plaftic hand of Education are very different—to accommodate the Apoftle's words—fome being to honour, fome to difhonour, precious ftones, gold, filver, brafs, lead—fome fit for the Preceptor's ufe, others modified

dified but one degree above torpid and inanimate matter. Wife and providential this variety! The natural and moral world is harmoniously confused—we fee order in variety—and partial evil is univerfal good. Superior intelligence is born to direct the machine—the lowest degree of it is born to drudge in turning its wheels. Distinguished genius is raised up for eminent ufefulnefs: thofe who are not bleffed with thefe talents are alfo fitted for ufefulnefs, though not for fuch extenfive ufefulnefs. All the intermediate orders, from the lowest up to the highest gradation of knowledge and difcernment, are wifely filled up—nothing but a divine hand could fcatter fo much beauty and elegance, fo much happinefs and good over civil and moral life, chequer fociety into fuch a pleafing and harmonious variety, and combine fuch infinite numbers of men of different talents, dif-

H 5 ferent

ferent taftes, different inclinations, into
one uniform and confiftent whole——
And it ought ever to be remembered,
that him, whom it hath pleafed God
to fignalize with diftinguifhed natural
abilities, and to impart to him thofe
intellectual talents and endowments
which few poffefs, he expects fhould
improve them in a worthy, credita-
ble, ufeful manner, and, by the dint
of affiduous culture and virtuous induftry, fhould render them peculiarly
ferviceable to the interefts of mankind. Ten talents are put into their
hand, for the improvement or mifimprovement of which they muft one
day be accountable. *Of him, to whom
much hath been given, fhall alfo much be
required.* A great and facred depofit
is gracioufly committed to their truft——
and they are expected to be faithful
ftewards of the *manifold* grace of God.
He who receives but one talent, if he
improve it in the beft manner Providence

dence enables him to do, is an infinitely worthier character than he, who
having received ten, a large splendid
treasure of the finest abilities, suffers it to
rust away by sloth and indolence. Now
he, who hath been blessed with the
largest portion of nature's selectest
gifts, and employs these eminent talents in that noblest of all ambition,
the godlike ambition of being exten-
sively useful, constitutes the highest
degree of attainment mentioned by
our Saviour—is the hundred fold, the
most exalted summit of human virtue. Inferior abilities and inferior
improvements correspond to the inferior degrees of produce here specified—the sixty and the thirty fold.

But there is not only a vast diver-
sity in the original genius, abilities and
talents of men, but there is as great
a difference with regard to favourable
opportunities for the culture and improvement

provement of their intellectual and moral powers. What a difference does a religious and liberal education make between one who hath enjoyed this bleſſing, and another, who has been deprived of it, though their mental abilities and powers by nature might have been originally equal! What an immenſe gradation between the acute philoſopher and the untutored peaſant, between cultivated civilized life, and ſavage uncivilized barbariſm! The gem may originally be of the ſame intrinſic worth—the difference is, whether it be ſuffered to lie in its rude, rough, uſeleſs ſtate, or whether the hand of education point and poliſh it, and make it beam forth in all its radiance and luſtre.

I hardly know a ſtronger motive to humility of mind, than this conſideration ſuggeſts. Do the ſuperior advantages and improvements of any one

one lead him to look down on those
below him with supercilious arrogance
and proud diſdain? What weakneſs
and wickedneſs! Thoſe perſons in
the ſtations he ſo much deſpiſes, per
haps received from Nature's hand the
ſame ſtrong natural abilities he him-
ſelf received—it may be, ſtronger—
and would perhaps have made a
greater proficiency in knowledge and
goodneſs than he hath done, had Providence ſeen fit to have favoured them
with the ſame opportunities. Many a
POPE and MILTON, many a LOCKE and
NEWTON, many a CLARKE and TIL-
LOTSON, are now drudging in the me-
nial occupations of life, who would
have riſen to their diſtinguiſhed fame
in the republic of Learning and Phi-
loſophy, had they been bleſſed with
their education and advantages for
the cultivation of their minds, the inveſtigation of truth and ſcience, and
the advancement of Literature, Theology

ology and Ethics. But to whom fewer
opportunities have been given, of him
will less be required. He whose situation and station in life enables him
only to bring forth the sixty fold, or
the thirty fold, is equally acceptable
to God with him who enjoys the greatest advantages, and makes but a *pro-
portional* improvement.

God is not a rigorous and unreason-
able master, reaping where he hath
not sown, gathering where he hath
not strown, and expecting the greatest
improvements where he hath given the
fewest talents. God only expects improvements in proportion to our advantages for improving. If we fill up
those circumstances and relations of
life, in which he hath fixed us, with
their proper duties, this is all that is
required of us. It matters little what
part is assigned us—the great concern
is, to execute that part well. Persons
in

in the lowest, obscurest spheres of life,
if devout and virtuous, are as much
the objects of the Divine approbation, as those who adorn the most envied and illustrious. It ought to be
the principal object, the solicitous
concern of every man, to maintain an
irreproachable character in every state
and scene of life——to be diligent and
faithful, sober and industrious——and
to make those improvements of his
time and talents, which his station ad-
mits, and God expects. *God is no re-
specter of persons; but in every* station,
he who feareth God, and does his duty,
is acceptable with God. The lowest
classes of life, those who are obliged to
support themselves and families by
manual labour, are precluded from
making any considerable improvements in Religion —— these therefore
ought to redeem that time which the
compassion of God to man hath con-
secrated and appropriated for public
instruc-

instruction and edification; and, instead of sleeping at home, rambling into the fields, or sauntering in public houses on the Lord's Day, God expects that they should frequent his House for the sacred purpose of obtaining that religious knowledge and instruction, which during the week they have so few opportunities of acquiring. Those, who are immersed in secular business, and engaged in care and commerce, are expected to be faithful and upright in their dealings, and to expend what few avocations they can redeem from their daily occupations, on improving their minds—but it is not required that they should make those advances in learning and erudition, in arts, sciences, or philosophy, or in the study of Morality and Religion, as the Nobleman, the Gentleman, and the Divine. From the former God expects, proportionally, the sixty fold and the

thirty

thirty fold—from the latter he expects an hundred fold, as he hath placed them in situations fo eminently propitious to diftinguifhed knowledge, public ufefulnefs, and extenfive good.

Here permit me to remark the very eminent advantages which they, whom God hath bleffed with fuperior opulence, enjoy for attaining the higheft degree of virtue mentioned in the Parable. Your riches are the diftinguifhed bounty of a Divine hand— but they are talents, for the ufe or abufe of which you muft very fhortly be accountable. Great are your advantages for doing good, and fcattering bleffings over human life—in relieving indigence, in raifing the drooping head of fuffering merit, in making poor diftreffed families the abode of happinefs and joy, in fuccouring the fatherlefs and widow in their affliction, in contributing to the

fupport

support of charitable Institutions, in encouraging learning and genius in necessitous circumstances — by these beneficent dispositions and actions, being a kind of Vicegerents and tutelar good Spirits under God, in making the sphere, in which you act, happy. Remember, where God in the course of his Providence hath sown with so bountiful and capacious an hand, he expects a proportionably rich and ample harvest. The produce of an hundred fold he expects from you—and you disappoint his reasonable expectations, when his generous soil and generous seed only yield the scanty, disproportionate pittance of twenty or thirty fold —Much more do you frustrate his Providence, and blast his designs, when, instead of making his distinguished bounty to you shine forth in the fair and heavenly fruits of public beneficence and usefulness, you steal
away

away from the view of the world with
thofe fplendid talents that have been
entrufted to you—tie them up in a nap-
kin—depofit them in a mean miferable hole of your own digging, whether it be your own congenial dirt,
or in the public funds—then live as
fome have lived, and will live, on the
intereft of the intereft of their immenfe fortunes—not the heart to give
a poor ftarving wretch, or a poor
ftarving family, the leaft mean pittance to cover their nakednefs, and
buy them a morfel of bread—or,
what is *almoft* as bad as this—but
is a *comparatively happy* perverfion,
as it circulates wealth—to keep a magnificent table fpread with every thing
that opulence can purchafe, imagination fancy, or art modify—to live in
luxury, fenfuality, epicurifm, pamper-
ing a frail dying body, and gratify-
ing a palled faftidious appetite with
every delicacy that ranfacked nature

ture can supply—and yet all this while
have the heart to repulse a poor wretch
that only solicits for the crumbs that
fall from the luxurious board, but is
denied.

To the honour of the present age
there are very few such characters.
The present age is distinguished above
all preceding ages for that spirit of
humanity, beneficence, and charity,
which is become generally fashionable—and this opulent City is de-
servedly illustrious, for its chearful
and generous contributions both to
public and private charities. This is
the proper use of riches—this is a way
of improving them, which redounds
to the glory of the original Donor, to
the happiness of mankind, and returns by a reflex act upon ourselves
in the noblest and divinest satisfactions.

This

This it is which constitutes this bringing forth fruit, respectively, from twenty to an hundred fold, or any of the intermediate gradations, according to the proportionate advantages with which God hath severally blessed us—the rich being expected to *abound* in good works, to be generous in their distributions—persons in the middle classes of life to live and act agreeably to their sphere —the poor to be sober, honest, and industrious—and all ranks and orders of society to adorn the doctrine of God their Saviour, and, by a patient continuance in well-doing, seek for glory, honour, and immortality.

Finally, we may clearly infer from these different gradations of religious and moral improvement here noted in the Parable, that there will be different degrees of future happiness, accommodated to the different improvements which men have made in this pro-

probationary state. This is agreeable
to the nature of things—to the equity
and justice of the divine moral government—and to the express declarations
of the holy scripture. Those happy
persons, whom not the pleasures of
youth, the temptations of mankind,
and the weakness incident to old age
have drawn aside from the paths of
virtue—who have overcome great
temptations — displayed illustrious
worth—and have steadily through life
persisted in a regular undeviating tenour of religion and goodness, shall
be advanced to a very exalted degree
of celestial blessedness, and be distinguished with an *exceeding great* and
eternal weight of glory. While o-
thers of inferior attainments shall be
proportionally entitled to inferior degrees of felicity. A just and good
God will surely advance those highest
who loved him the soonest, and served
him the longest. Those who spent
their

their youth and riper years in fenfual
courfes, and afterwards repented and
reformed——for example, at thirty, or
forty, or fifty—will not enjoy the fame
eminent degrees of blifs as fhall fignal-
lize thofe who have expended the
bloom and prime of their days in
worthy and laudable purfuits, and who
have maintained a fpotlefs irreproachable character through all the fucceffive ftages and changing fcenes of
life.

Virtue rifes in proportion to the
oppofition it overcomes, and to the
inviolable principles and active goodnefs it difplays. Many a virtuous
Heathen will be advanced many degrees above infinite numbers of Chriftians, who were bleffed with fewer
advantages for religious and moral
improvement, yet made a much better ufe of the little light and knowledge

ledge they enjoyed, than Christians do,
of their singular privileges.

In my Father's house, says our Lord,
there are many mansions—many apart-
ments fitted up for the reception of
persons of different improvements.
The prophet Daniel, describing future happiness, says : *Those who are
wise shall shine as the brightness of the
firmament, but those who,* besides their
personal virtue, turn *many to righteouf-
ness, as the stars for ever and ever*——
And the Apostle Paul expressly affures us, that the beatified spirits shall
have as striking gradations of glory as
we observe between the splendour of
the sun and moon, or between one star
and another.

APPLICATION.

How should this consideration fire
us with Christian ambition ! How
should these glorious prospects stimu-
late

late us to excell, and so to run that we may obtain. Heaven hath rewards equal to the most consummate virtue we can display. The greater our virtue here, the greater our felicity hereafter. The nearer we approach God here in doing good, the nearer we shall be stationed to his celestial throne in the regions of immortality. Having therefore these animating promises, let us be stedfast and immoveable, always abounding in the work of the Lord; forasmuch as we know, that our labour in the Lord shall not be in vain.

I conclude with this one important sentiment, which I leave to your serious consideration; and I beg of God, that none of the pleasures, follies, and cares of life may ever erase it from your remembrance: Strive not merely to secure future happiness, but to secure eminent degrees of future happiness.

I
S E R-

S E R M O N VII.

M A T. T H. xiii. 9.

He that hath ears to hear, let him hear.

WITH great vehemence and the moſt pathetic earneſtneſs one may juſtly ſuppoſe our Saviour to have pronounced theſe words at the concluſion of this inſtructive Parable of the Sower——and of this circumſtance St. Luke, in recording

I 2

the

the fame Parable, informs us : *When he had faid thefe things, he* CRIED, *He that hath ears to hear, let him hear.* This is a form of fpeaking which often occurs in the Evangelifts, and which we frequently find our Saviour importunately uttered after the delivery of the moft folemn and momentous truths. I fhall endeavour in this difcourfe minutely to illuftrate our Lord's defign in this addrefs, and offer to your ferious attention fuch remarks as the words obvioufly fuggeft.

In the firft place, they appear evidently calculated to excite and fix mens attention to what our Saviour delivered. Such a laconic, awakening fentence, vehemently pronounced and addreffed to the audience, after the recital of an inftructive Parable, or at the end of one of his heavenly difcourfes, delivered by a Perfon, who affumed a divine authority, and with

with a folemnity, that fpoke his own
dignity, and the fublimity and moment of the doctrines he taught, muft
have all its effect—awe every power—
roufe every faculty—and ftrike every
heart. With what irrefragable force
muft fuch a warm, pathetic, fenten-
tious conclufion feal the inftruction
delivered, imprefs it on the heart, and
powerfully excite the mind to revolve
the truths it had juft heard, and make
them the fubject of its moft ferious
and deliberate regards. They were a
folemn appeal to the underftanding of
his audience, carefully to examine his
pretenfions to the character he affumed
as a Teacher fent from God, and to
confult their own hearts, whether the
doctrines and morals he taught were
worthy fuch a commiffion, or, if believed and practifed, would be perfective of the glory and happinefs of
human nature.

The

The folemn paufe, that enfued after the empaffioned pronunciation of
this ftriking fentence, would make
the hearer diftinctly and deliberately
go over again the feveral particulars
of the Parable or Difcourfe—ferioufly
weigh their importance—fix his ideas
to their facred moment—and bring
home to his bofom their great end
and defign. It would be a folemn
interval, in which all the hearer's
thoughts would be deeply engaged—
for example—in confidering the reafonablenefs of the doctrines he had
heard—in tracing their correfpondence
to the law of truth—in reflecting how
much his happinefs was interefted in
them—in comparing the fublimity of
the doctrines with the heavenly authority of the Perfon who delivered
them—in fummoning all his mental
and moral powers to retain thefe celeftial inftructions—deliberately refolv-
ing in the mean time to carry home
　　　　　　　　　　　　　　a warm,

a warm, affecting sense of these things, and give a circumstantial detail of every particular to their parents, their wives, their children, their brothers, their relations—charging their memory to engrave these divine truths in living characters on their hearts—and determining that nothing, nothing should ever efface them from their remembrance.

From this concise, vehement address, one may infer the spirited manner in which our Saviour preached. One may conclude from this, that our Lord delivered his public instructions with a warmth and pathos equal to the dignity and moment of the truths they contained. With what holy rage and divine indignation does he tear off the hypocrite's specious mask, and shew the world the turpitude and deformity that lurked behind! With what spirited declamation does he pro-

nounce

nounce his woes upon the Scribes and Pharisees, and upon the most dignified and illustrious among that abandoned people, satirizing their dissimulation, avarice, ostentation, pride, superstition, and unfeeling inhumanity, with the most sacred zeal and fervour, and in the warmest strains of heart-inspired eloquence remonstrating against their abominable corruptions in doctrine, and abominable profligacy in practice, exposing their little trifling ceremonious observances to palliate their vices, and atone for the want of personal holiness—— to excite detestation and horror, publickly recounting the flagrant enormities of this demure race of hypocrites, as the Jewish nation in that age most certainly was, with a vehemence which the orators of Greece and Rome never surpassed. Let any person read the twenty-third chapter of St. Matthew's Gospel, and judge whether

our

our Saviour fuffered men to flumber
in their vices——whether he tamely fuffered the manners and principles of
thofe abandoned times to pafs uncen-
fured——or whether his public difcourfes were delivered in a dull, fpiritlefs,
unanimated manner. Our Saviour
was in earneft——Would to God all the
Preachers of his Religion were infpired
with the fame holy fervour and facred
earneftnefs! It was his meat and drink
to do the Will of God, to exterminate
errour, and eftablifh truth, to pluck
the hoary venerable tyrant Superfti-
tion from that throne he had ufurped
fo long, and to erect an everlafting
empire of true Religion——and fuch a
commiffion as this he would not execute in a carelefs, negligent, perfunctory manner. It was his facred ambition to emancipate the human mind
from that cruel flavery in which it had
been detained fo long, to free it from
the ignominious fetters of falfe fyftem

and

and prejudice, to vindicate it into the glorious liberty of truth and virtue, to diſſolve mens ſanguine attachment to ſecular intereſt, to inflame their minds with the glorious proſpect of immortality—and can it be ſuppoſed that he, who was purpoſely delegated from heaven by the Supreme to re-form the world, to publiſh theſe ſacred truths, and to execute this great commiſſion, would deliver it with un-feeling coldneſs, neither affected him-ſelf, nor deſirous to affect others?

How proper is the animated lan-guage in my text, *He that hath ears to hear, let him hear*, from the lips of one who appeared among men inveſt-ed with a divine authority, and who challenged the world's attention to the meſſage which God Almighty deputed him to proclaim? Who could ſuffer ſupine negligence and liſtleſsneſs to ſeize his ſpirit, and be-numb

numb his powers, when the great
G o d was fpeaking to him by his
Ambaſſador and Apoſtle. Who
could be an inattentive hearer, when
one, who exhibited the ſtrongeſt
proofs of the dignity of his perſon,
the authority of his pretenſions, and
the credibility of his doctrines, was
affectionately expoſtulating with him,
by all the authority of his commiſſion, and with all the energy that
truth can inſpire, to relinquiſh errour, abandon vice, and embrace Religion?——And muſt not theſe exhorta-
tions to repentance, amendment, and
holineſs, be urged with an importu-
nate and ſacred ardour that no well-
diſpoſed mind could reſiſt? —— muſt
not ſuch ſpirited addreſſes as this in
the text flow with a warmth and fer-
vency which ſpoke them the genuine
dictates of an heart that felt their importance, and was painfully conſcious
what depended on mens' wilful rejec-
tion

tion of them. The flame of devotion and piety, which was kindled in our Saviour's bosom, animated all his discourses. *From the abundance of his heart his mouth spoke.* His language received its spirit and force from the zeal which prompted it. His soul was penetrated with the love of God and of mankind, and his pathetic discourses shew us the strength of these divine principles. Language is but the expression of the heart—the overflowings of a person's inward sensibilities. It is the heart which gives animation to the diction and to the manner of a public speaker. The heart appears visible through the interposing veil, and leads us to judge of the degree in which it is actuated to do good. This rule applied to our Saviour's discourses, will make his heart appear in a very amiable light. We shall see from what sincerity his expressions flowed — how dear our

ever-

everlafting interefts were to him—
with what facred love of truth and
holinefs his bofom glowed—what genuine compaffion and love engaged
him to reafon and expoftulate with
men—and what holy ardour caught
his fpirit and wrapped his powers,
when he was publickly delivering his
divine difcourfes, and affectionately
urging men, by all the perfuafive arguments that could affect their underftandings, or ftrike their paffions,
and with all the vehemence that truth
could infpire, or a meffenger from
God employ, to repent, to reform,
and embrace that Religion, which had
the great God for its Author, and
would infallibly put them in poffeffion
of everlafting bleffednefs. From fuch
a mind, infpired with the dignity of
fuch a fubject, flowed the animated
expreffions of the text—and they folemnly call upon every rational mind
deliberately to confider the authority
which

which spoke them, the principles
which dictated them, the pathos which
distinguishes them, and the importance and moment of those preceding
discourses, to which they are sub-
joined.

This is a very strong and emphatical appeal to the reason and understanding of men. Our Lord rests the
truths he published upon the impartial decisions of reason. He appeals to
its tribunal, and refers men for the
nature and excellence of his Religion
to its sovereign verdict. Christ does
not force and obtrude his doctrines
upon us. He puts no coercive re-
straint upon the native freedom and
liberty of our minds. The sacrifice
of our understanding is not a victim,
which our great High-priest requires
us to immolate at the foot of his altar. It was never the intention of
our Lawgiver, that we should resign
our

our understanding in matters of Religion——should exercise our rational and intellectual powers in every thing except in matters of Religion. It is the unrivalled glory of Christianity, that it is a rational Religion——worthy that great Being to give, who is pure and perfect Reason——and worthy the reception of such a creature as man, whose distinguishing glory it is to be endued with reason. Christianity never contradicts right reason——it illustrates and confirms it. Its truths and principles are consonant to its genuine dictates——and they mutually corroborate and elucidate each other. Christianity is a rational institution —— its precepts and doctrines are such as reason approves——it lodges the appeal for its reasonableness and credibility to our own heart——it can be vindicated and demonstrated upon the unerring principles of reason——and so long as man continues capable of exercising

ing his rational powers, fo long will
Chriftianity approve itfelf to every
virtuous, well-difpofed mind, to be
*the wifdom of God and the power of
God*, and to have every internal evidence that can evince it to be an expli-
cit revelation from the God of truth.
How often do we find our Saviour
and his Apoftles appealing to men for
the *reafonablenefs* of what they deliver
—fufpending the decifion upon the
faithful genuine dictates of their own
breafts—ufing no compulfive, violent, arbitrary methods, but openly
exhibiting the evidences of Religion
before the human mind, and generoufly leaving it to draw the conclufion.

Our Saviour's miracles were wrought
without any oftentatious parade. They
were accompanied with no vain-glo-
rious rhodomontade, or with that ful-
fome pomp and vociferation, with
which

which impoftors, in all ages, difplay their falfe, fictitious miracles, and impofe upon the credulity of the deluded multitude. The miracles of our Saviour were performed with modefty and filence——and the facts were left to fpeak their own language——And fuch amazing operations, making the lame to walk, the blind to fee, and the dead to live, would fpeak, in reafon's ear, in more ftrong and emphatic accents, than all the declamations of all the orators in the world, had they been all affembled upon the occafion.

The public difcourfes alfo of our Saviour were addreffed to the human heart, to the principles of mens reafon and underftanding——the doctrines, duties, and difcoveries were fairly and openly propounded, and they were left to reafon concerning them, to bring them to the native ftandard of their judgment

ment and moral difcernment—Chrift being defirous that men fhould be the rational believers of his Gofpel—converts from principle and mental conviction—fully perfuaded in their own minds that Chriftianity was founded upon argument and evidence, and was a revelation from the infinite Source of truth and wifdom, in every refpect worthy its great and good Author, and perfective of the higheft dignity and glory of the rational character. Take away reafon, and you fink man to a level with the brutes below him—to a level, did I fay—you degrade him many degrees below the beafts that perifh—many degrees below the fagacious horfe and the *half-reafoning* elephant. How do we know that the Scripture is a divinely-infpired Book but by our reafon? Extinguifh the light of Reafon, and with profane, irreverent hands you extinguifh that Lamp, which the great

Father

Father of lights hath fixed and kindled in your breasts: Vilify and depreciate Reason, and you revile and vilify the noblest emanation that reaches you from the supreme Source of wisdom. God is dishonoured, when you dishonour that which makes you what you are—a creature highly exalted in the scale of being, the lord of the creation, dignified with many vast and enlarged capacities, impressed with the image of God, and distinguished with faculties capable of receiving greater and greater improvements in knowledge and happiness through all the revolving ages of an endless immortality.

The reason I carry in my bosom is as much an emanation from God as any external system of divine truths can be. God does not give one light to extinguish another, but to aid, improve, and strengthen it. When

When the eye of Reason had been obfcured by vice, and it was found in-
fufficient to reform and reclaim a
corrupt and depraved world, God in-
terpofed, and in this *fulnefs of time*
fent his Son to feek and to fave that
which was loft, and to recover men
to liberty, virtue, and happinefs.
Though human reafon could of itfelf
never have contrived and planned fuch
a fcheme as the Gofpel, and after all
its moft generous exertions could never have furnifhed fuch a fyftem of
Religion and Morals, fo clearly delivered, enforced by fuch an authority,
embellifhed with fo many fhining examples, illuftrated with fuch a fublimity of doctrine, replete with fuch
animating encouragements, and recommended to the love and acceptance of mankind by the beautiful
united affemblage of every argument
and evidence that can win our affent
and eftablifh our belief of it—though
human

human reafon, after all its efforts, could never have contrived and executed fuch a plan, yet, when difcovered, it appears perfectly congruous and analogous to all the dictates and principles of Reafon——it approves itfelf to all the rational and moral powers, and inftead of overwhelming the light which God by nature poured upon the mind, and rendering it worthlefs and ufelefs, it only contributes to make it break forth with fuperior radiance, directs its enquiries with greater certainty, purges the mental eye more effectually from the films of errour, and, by the additional rays fhed upon it, makes it to fee its duty and happinefs in a clearer, ftronger point of view, than ever before it beheld it. Chriftianity is the perfection of all Religion, becaufe it is the perfection of Reafon—— and becaufe it hath improved and exalted the human mind infinitely beyond

yond any other Religion the world
ever faw. The pathetic language
therefore of our Saviour in the text,
which is of fuch frequent occurrence,
is an appeal to the reafon, understanding, and judgment of mankind
in regard to the nature and genius of
the Chriftian Religion.——Whether it
be founded upon Reafon, or whether
it be an infult and outrage upon Reafon—he holds up before the virtuous
well-difpofed mind a faithful picture
of his Religion; and as fuch a mind
is qualified to judge, leaves it to its
natural fentiments and reflections on
the fair and perfect piece.

This phrafe further implies, that
we fhould diligently employ our rational and moral faculties in the ftudy
of Truth and Virtue. The true meaning of this ftrong, figurative, oriental
expreffion, *He that hath ears to hear,
let him hear,* in modern language is
this :

this : Let him, that is endowed with rational and intellectual powers, carefully cultivate and improve them in the investigation of Truth, and the acquisition of sacred Knowledge. It was never the design of our Creator, when he furnished us with such abilities, capable of such vast attainments, that we should suffer them to lie dormant and neglected, useless to the world and to ourselves.

God in his Providence hath opened before us a boundless field of science, and he hath given us the power of ranging its ample circle, and culling its selectest flowers. The excursions of the mind are unlimited——it transports itself in a moment to the remotest regions and kingdoms of the world—— is a spectator of their government, manners, and customs——and sits as judge on their religion, polity, and various regulations. It traverses the pathlefs fields of fpace, attends the fun, moon, and planets, in their revolutions, fixes and determines their periods, and by the amazing dint of philofophical fpeculation, for many years to come, accurately predicts the various changes that will affect thefe immenfe bodies. The ocean it explores, inveftigates the nature of the tides, the laws of gravity, the properties of the animal and vegetable creation, the principles of the human mind, and in every direction traverfes thofe moft extenfive regions, which Hiftory, Philofophy, and Theology fpread before it. God hath opened before us the two great volumes of Nature and Revelation, replete with inexhauftible treafures of knowledge and wifdom of the moft ufeful kind, and beft adapted to adorn and exalt the mind—and he expects that we fhould carefully perufe the fair and heavenly pages of thefe books, and

that

that we fhould embellifh and enrich
our minds with a fplendid, ufeful fund
of facred inftruction. We fhould be
unjuft to the great and good Author
of our intellectual powers, if we did
not affiduoufly cultivate and improve
them, and carefully exercife them,
according to our refpective opportunities, in the ftudy and purfuit of
every thing that may gain us the reputation of being fenfible and intelligent,
as well as virtuous and good. In all
our enquiries Truth fhould be our
great object and aim. To this all our
ftudies fhould be directed. When we
read the book of Nature, or the book
of Revelation, this is the one great
fcope to which we are to tend—this
is the facred paffion, with which our
breafts fhould be incurably fmitten.
——the love of truth fhould animate
and infpirit us through all the difficulties that lie in the road to it.

K   And

And what ought to have infinite weight with us, and ftimulate us in all our refearches, is, That God will illuminate a mind thus worthily employed, will aid and direct it in its enquiries, will guard it from every deftructive errour, and irradiate it with the clear perception and knowledge of every thing conducive to its prefent felicity and future bleffednefs. What can be a greater encouragement to us, to animate us in the ftudy of the Scriptures, and in the fearch of Truth, than the confideration that there is a Being of infinite wifdom ever prompt and difpofed to enlighten our imperfect minds, who with paternal fmiles ftands ready from his uplifted hand to throw upon the labouring mind fuch heavenly light as will difpel the darknefs of prejudice and ignorance——who will ftrengthen the mental eye to fee Truth in all her celeftial form and infinite attractions——and if honeft in our

our enquiries, and folely intent upon the improvement of our minds in every thing amiable and laudable, will invigorate our intellectual powers with his divine influence.' `He, who pervades the fpirit, can enlighten it—he, who has immediate accefs to the mind, can irradiate its powers, and fortify and direct its abilities. *If any lack wifdom, let him afk it of God.*

In all our enquiries after Truth, therefore, let us never forget our abfolute dependence upon the Deity, to whofe goodnefs we are indebted for all the knowledge we are capacitated to acquire—who originally gave us our faculties, and all the means and opportunities we enjoy for improving them—and above all, in the purfuit of religious knowledge, let our application conftantly be made, with the devouteft homage and reverence, to the great indefectible Source of light

K 2 and

and .Fountain of truth, who giveth
liberally and upbraideth not. Let us
make the wifeft and beft ufe of our
fugitive moments. Let us conftantly
be occupied in purfuits that are ho-
nourable, decent, and laudable. Let
us diligently improve the powers,
which God hath given us on purpofe
that we fhould improve them. Let
us cherifh an infatiable paffion for facred Truth and ufeful Knowledge, and
a fortitude and firmnefs in profeffing
and publifhing the truth. Let us
make the Holy Scriptures our delight
and our ftudy. Let us eftablifh and
confirm every moral principle and virtuous difpofition—and by this worthy
employment of our reafon, by this re-
putable improvement of our time and
talents, and by the affiduous, unwearied cultivation of every thing amiable
and excellent, let us maintain the
dignity of our ftation as men, the dignity of our characters as Chriftians,
and

and effectually accomplish the grand
and glorious defign, for which God
endowed us with reafon, infpired into
us the principle of immortality, and
called us into being amidft fuch diftinguifhed advantages.

The language of my text is commanding and authoritative. After
our Saviour had delivered his Sermon
on the mount, it is obferved that the
people were *aftonifhed at his doctrine*—
and the reafon affigned for the effect
his inftructions produced, is, becaufe
he *taught* them as one *having authority*—he delivered his inftructions with
an air of Divine dignity, which infpired reverence, and commanded attention—*and not as the Scribes*—not in
that carelefs, indolent, unaffecting
manner in which the Jewifh Clergy
taught the people. Our Saviour fpake
with a majefty that fhewed his commiffion from God—by the awful fo-

K 3 lemnity

lemnity of his manner, diction, accent, air, action, he reigned over the audience, and struck them with the last astonishment. The powers he displayed were irresistible—they penetrated through all the folds of the heart, and awed every power and passion into admiration and reverence. The thunder and lightning of DEMOSTHENES's eloquence, as the ancients characterized it, were nothing to the wonderful effects of our Saviour's authoritative, heaven-inspired oratory. It subdued every virtuous heart, captivated every virtuous affection, piercing to the *dividing asunder of the joints and marrow*, and intimately pervading the thoughts and intents of the heart. He came from heaven, cloathed with a divine authority—and he spake and taught as one invested with this dignity. His discourses did not perplex and embarrass the auditors with philosophical difficulties,

culties, curious speculative researches, elaborate metaphysical disquisitions, and with solutions of such arduous subjects in Philosophy and Morals, that raised more objections than they removed. He brought PHILOSOPHY from heaven, dressed in a plain, artless, undisguised manner, and exhibited her divine form to the world, to strike men with the most sacred passion and love for her. His Philosophy is not replete with infinite subtilties and inane refinements——it is a simple, clear, intelligible system, stamped with the most venerable and sacred authority.

You have an example of the commanding, authoritative manner, in which our Saviour delivered his discourses, in several parts of his Sermon on the mount. *You have heard that it was said in old time,* &c.——*but I say unto you.*

A well-

A well-attested *divine* authority was greatly wanting to give the precepts of *human* philosophy their proper seal and sanction. Philosopher contradicted philosopher, and one school of wisdom taught sect and system quite repugnant to another. The Platonic, the Peripatetic, the Stoic, the Epicurean philosophy widely differed. Where must the common people of Heathen countries go for instruction? Their wise and eminent sages were divided— their assertions and names did not give their systems any proper authority. Some of their systems were atheistical and detestable—some visionary and romantic. What power had they to reclaim and reform the world? What authority could they plead, except the authority of their idle speculative dreams and ideal reveries, to enforce their doctrines, and gain them a general reception among men? What good effects did the Philosophy of *Plato* or the

the Offices of *Cicero* produce on the lives and morals of the bulk of mankind? We find that most of the Philosophers and Lawgivers of antiquity were obliged to have recourse to pious frauds, and to falsify and counterfeit the authority of some of their Deities, in order to give their laws and injunctions a proper moment and weight with the *people*.

How infinitely therefore hath the Christian Religion the advantage of these motley heterogeneous bodies of human Philosophy, which is sealed with the signet of the great God, and ratified and confirmed by the most venerable and sacred authority of him, who is the image of the invisible God.

Well might our Saviour, therefore, who was delegated to this lower world to publish the Will of God, and appeared among us invested with this

most

moft illuftrious office and character, with an air of authority, with heavenly majefty beaming from his looks, in every gefture dignity and love, ftretch forth his hands over the world, raife his voice, and utter this commanding language : He who is formed capable of hearing and receiving facred truth, let him attend to the inftructions of my Religion. He that defpifeth me, defpifeth not me, but HIM who fent me. I am come in my FATHER's Name. The Doctrine is not mine, but HIS that fent me. A Religion therefore that hath GOD for its Author, and was publifhed under the fanction of his Name and Authority, claims our reverence——and the dignity of its illuftrious Publifher fhould moft powerfully enforce its great Truths and Principles upon our hearts.

APPLL

APPLICATION.

These words are also expressive of the infinite moment and importance of those things to which we are commanded to give this diligent and serious attention. Death and Judgment, Heaven and Hell, are before us. Everlasting happiness, or everlasting destruction, depends on our attention or inattention to these great concerns. Who would allow himself to trifle when his happiness to all eternity, or the total loss of it to all eternity, is at stake? Who would not be all ear, all attention, when God is speaking, Christ expostulating, and Angels waiting to see whether we embrace or reject these friendly admonitions? Our everlasting welfare is here suspended. Happiness or misery are proposed to our choice. According as we improve or misimprove this transi-

tranfitory uncertain life, fo will our everlafting condition be unalterably fixed.   Chrift and his Apoftles do not mean to footh us in our foft falfe dreams of fenfual joy—to fpeak peace to us, while we are traverfing a circle of every gay amufement and folly. They mean to awaken us from thefe delufive, fatal flumbers, by founding in Reafon's ear, Repent and reform : obey the Gofpel : *Awake, thou that fleepeft, and arife from the dead, and Chrift fhall give thee light :* The night of life is far fpent, the day is at hand ; the morning of the refurrection begins to dawn : now is the accepted time, behold, now is the day of falvation : He, that hath ears to hear, let him attend to the inftructions of Jefus, and the doctrines of eternal life, while God gives him an opportunity of attending to them.

Eternal

Eternal life is no poetic fiction. The Christian's Heaven is no Pagan Elysium, or Mohammedan Paradise. It is a great and glorious reality—no ideal world — no region of sensual softness and voluptuousness insatiable. It is as pure and undefiled, as sacred and holy, as the presence of God and Christ and Angels and good Spirits can make it. Nothing but holiness shall ever be admitted within its sacred precincts. It will require all the care we can employ, all the time we can improve, and all the virtue we can cultivate and attain, to fit us for its blessed mansions.

Let us attend to these truths—let nothing ever erase them from our remembrance. It is at our peril we reject them. The blame, if we repulse them, is only ours. Our guilt, and our loss of immortality—these only can be charged upon ourselves. We

were

were acceffary to it, if ever fuch a dire event fhould ever happen to any of us, which God of his infinite mercy avert.

While Chrift therefore is fpeaking to us, warning us of our danger, expoftulating with us, addreffing himfelf to our reafon, underftanding, and heart, let us hear, obey, and live. Let us not confider the Book, which contains thefe admonitions, as merely a Book of ancient Hiftory—a Book of amufement to kill a vacant hour on a Sunday evening—but let us reflect that thefe things are written that we fhould believe on the Name of the Son of God, and that believing, and acting as if we believed, we might through his Name be wife, and happy to all eternity.

Finally, Let us impartially examine and compare our hearts with the defcriptive

4

fcriptive reprefentations, which our
Saviour in the preceding Parable hath
given of its various ftates. In our
moments of retirement, in an hour of
cool reflection, let us lay our hand
on our heart, and in the prefence of
the great Searcher of them, folemnly
afk ourfelves thefe queftions : Is this
heart, like the hard, beaten, impenetrable furface, on which the word of
God fell, but could make no impreffion, and which the fowls of the air,
every vain, fantaftic, airy pleafure,
with voracious greedinefs picked up
as moft delicious prey, the moment
it fell——Is this heart covered with a
flight mold, with impenetrable rocks
lurking juft beneath its furface, capable of bringing no virtuous refolution, no defigns of amendment and
ufefulnefs to any maturity——Is this
heart choked with the baleful weeds
of covetoufnefs and worldly-mindednefs, and will fuffer nothing holy or

heavenly

heavenly to grow and flourish under its poisonous shade—Or can I say, that I enjoy the greatest of all blessings, GOODNESS OF HEART—that I have an heart disposed to every good word and work—disposed to cherish every kind affection, cultivate and perfect every Christian virtue, and, by the fair and heavenly fruits that flourish in its genial soil, blessing me with the delectable prospect of reaping a rich harvest of eternal glory. Let it be our principal concern to govern our passions, to rectify our heart, to improve our time, to extirpate every evil, to cherish every good disposition; and in the uniform, undeviating course of a virtuous, useful, and truly Christian life, prepare for death and eternity, and God will be with us and bless us in all the changing scenes of this life, and finally crown us with eminent degrees of happiness in the realms of immortality.

THE

THE

NATURE and DESIGN

OF THE

CHRISTIAN RELIGION.

ADVERTISEMENT.

THE three following Sermons having an intimate connection with the subject of the preceding Discourses, I hope the Reader will receive them with candour, and peruse them with edification.

EDWARD HARWOOD.

SERMON VIII.

GAL. v. 22, 23.

The fruit of the Spirit is love, joy, peace, long-suffering, gentleness, goodness, faith, meekness, temperance: against such there is no law.

CHristianity is the perfection of all Religion. The best interest of mankind hath this divine system consulted. Its ultimate design and tendency is apparently to carry human nature

nature to the higheſt ſummit of happineſs. All its precepts, doctrines,
and ſanctions, are calculated to produce the higheſt virtue and felicity of
human kind, and to ſpread an amiable
and delectable ſcene of univerſal harmony, concord, and love among all
its profeſſors. It is ſuch a Religion,
as is infinitely worthy of a Being to
give, whoſe darling attribute is Benevolence and Love—and ſuch a Religion, as is infinitely worthy the reception of a creature, whoſe higheſt happineſs reſults from the cultivation of
benevolence and love.

When our bleſſed Saviour was
uſhered into this ſcene of being, the
heavenly choirs, in rapturous and ac-
cordant ſtrains, repeated, PEACE,
PEACE, GOOD WILL TOWARDS MEN.
This ſhort triumphal Ode, ſung by
theſe angelic hoſts at our Saviour's
nativity, is deſcriptive of the genius
and

and nature of this Divine Religion, which is by way of diftinction ftyled, THE GOSPEL OF PEACE—and whofe cardinal characteriftic virtue is good will and univerfal charity.

When our Lord's Difciples, tranf-ported with a furious zeal againft the inhabitants of a Samaritan village, which had refufed their Mafter the rites of hofpitality, and prohibited his entrance into the town, importu-nately defired him by a miracle to command fire from heaven to con-fume thefe ftubborn aud abufive wretches——our Lord reproved them for the fanguinary fpirit they difco-vered——he turned and rebuked them, faying, *Ye know not what manner of fpirit ye are of* —— You are perfect ftrangers to the genius of my Reli-gion, and the fpirit it breathes. The Son of God came not to infpire men with principles of malevolence, cru-elty,

elty, and revenge ; but to fill the human bosom with sentiments of love, amity, mutual forbearance, affection, harmony, and charity.

The intention of this blessed Religion is best seen by contrasting it with other Religions, which have made pretensions to a Divine Revelation. Read the Turkish Koran—every page is stained with blood. Murder and bloodshed are the means which this *divine* volume, the Koran, sanctifies in propagating its doctrines. Mohammedism is founded in conquest and empire, and justifies its professors in wading through oceans of human blood to its erection and establishment in the world. God, says this Impostor, commissioned Jesus Christ to give men a system of Divine Laws, which he endeavoured to spread and promulgate among mankind by the dint of their intrinsic amiableness, and by

2   by

By means of moral fuafion, mildnefs, and lenity—but when thefe gentle methods were eventually found to be ineffectual, God authorifed me to propagate his Religion by compulfion, by conqueft, and to ufe more cogent arguments with mankind, fince pacific perfuafions were totally inadequate and fruitlefs. In confequence of which the Religion of Mahomet, which hath been propagated to fuch a prodigious extent, hath entirely reverfed the words of my text—for the fruit of that fpirit, which the Koran breathes, is rage, rancour, fury, animofity, revenge, devaftation, murder, the infernal paffion of making converts by fire and fword.

How diametrically oppofite to fuch a temper and difpofition are the amiable and godlike principles of the Religion of Jefus!—What a ftriking contraft this to the character of the

L bene-

benevolent Jefus, who was meek and
lowly in heart, the friend of all mankind, in whofe bofom every thing
dwelt that was humane, benevolent,
and divine, and who left this ever-
memorable Sentence as a Leffon to
all his followers, in all future ages:
By THIS SHALL ALL MEN KNOW THAT
YOU ARE MY DISCIPLES, IF YOU LOVE
ONE ANOTHER.

It is greatly to be lamented, and
the thought cannot fail to infpire a
ferious mind with generous pity and
indignation, That Chriftians, in all
ages of the Church, fhould have
fo miferably departed from the fpirit
of the Gofpel. I am forry to make
the following remark ; but, alas ! it
is but too juft and obvious——That
there is no fpecies of hiftory, which a
benevolent, humane well-wifher of
mankind reads with lefs pleafure than
Ecclefiaftical Hiftory. It is very dif-
agreeable,

agreeable, when a perfon hath read the hiftory of our Lord, and obferves, as every one muft do, what ftrict injunctions our Redeemer again and again urges upon all his followers—— repeating thefe admonitions in every difcourfe——upon every occafion——*to love one another——A new commandment I give unto you, That you love one another——*It is very unpleafing and ungrateful, when one confiders thefe ufeful directions, to turn one's reflections to the *fubfequent* times, and fee how thefe moft folemn admonitions of our great Mafter were fulfilled by thofe who valued themfelves upon being the profeffors of his Religion. Had our bleffed Saviour left this precept on record to all his followers : *A new commandment I give unto you, That you hate one another——*how could it have been better fulfilled than what it hath been——than

what

what it hath been from the third Century to the present day?

One shudders to think what seas of human blood have been spilt in what are called *Religious Wars*. What dreadful massacres did the various and discordant sects and parties of Christians alternately exercise one upon another in the respective reigns of CONSTANTINE's Successors——burning villages, storming towns, pillaging rich and fertile countries, and putting all, without distinction, to the sword, who did not think exactly as they did in certain metaphysical, speculative controversies, which they themselves, who exercised these cruelties, freely acknowledged to be incomprehensible and unintelligible.

The evident design of the Gospel is to unite men one to another——and mutual charity was designed to be the great

great bond and cement of this union. But different professions of Christians have, in general, lived and acted, as if their common Religion was intended to set men at ~~irreconcilable~~ variance and the remotest distance one from another. The Gospel's great aim is, to conciliate mens' affections one to another——if one might judge of its nature and tendency from the reciprocal conduct of its several denominations towards each other, one would conclude, its purpose and end was to inspire men with black resentment, implacable discord, and uncharitable animosities against each other.

One would think that our blessed Saviour and his Apostles had these unhappy scenes in view, which afterwards happened in the Christian Church, when they so earnestly and importunately entreated and conjured Christians, by every affecting argu-

ment

ment and motive, to cultivate mutual affection, concord, and love, one towards another——And there is hardly any thing that fhews the amiable Religion of Jefus in a more engaging, endearing light, than that it is by no means chargeable with thofe dire difcords and uncharitable controverfies its profeffors have kindled——that it is by no means chargeable with thofe deftructive flames of war and fcenes of bloodfhed which the worft paffions of men have raifed——that thefe are unhappy events it never defigned, but, on the contrary, was publifhed to mankind to fupprefs and extinguifh ——and that, inftead of inflating men with arrogance and oftentation, and of blowing up their worft paffions into fury, envy, bitternefs, malice, and mutual diffenfion, its fole ftudy, and grand, capital, primary defign is, to reconcile men one to another, by means of *one* common union, *one* common

mon Religion, *one* common Redeemer —and to inspire all, who name the sacred Name of Jesus, with the moſt generous benevolence, with mutual concord, and univerſal charity and love. *The fruit of the Spirit is love, joy, peace, long-ſuffering, goodneſs, faith, meekneſs.*

The bleſſed effects of the Goſpel are here diſtinctly enumerated. By the *fruits of the Spirit* are meant the genuine product of Chriſtianity. Theſe amiable virtues are the very eſſence and ſpirit of the Goſpel—they are its ſupreme, unrivalled excellence and glory—they are the pure and ſacred ſtreams, which flow from this divine fountain. When the Goſpel is imbibed and cordially embraced, it produces theſe fair and bleſſed fruits as naturally as any Cauſe produceth its Effect. Peace and love and meekneſs and gentleneſs and charity are the

L 4

fruit

fruit by which the nature of the tree is eminently diſtinguiſhed. *A good tree bringeth forth good fruit.* Virtuous, benevolent principles ſhine in virtuous, benevolent actions. There is an inſeparable connection betwixt them. If the heart, the fountain of goodneſs, be virtuous, the inferior affections will be virtuous. If that Religion, which is the rule and guide of a man's life and conduct, be founded in the happineſs of ſociety and the holineſs of individuals, whereever it is cordially received and adopted, it will beam forth in all its native ſplendour and divine luſtre, in the diſpoſitions, affections, and morals of thoſe who believe it to be divinely authenticated.

There were great numbers, I believe, of devout, holy, and virtuous Heathens—but the public Religion, which they eſpouſed, had a flagrant tendency

tendency to render them to the laſt degree depraved and corrupt. For what were their Gods, whom they adored? what were the grand objects of their worſhip?——Monſters of cruelty, luſt, and drunkenneſs. Had many of the Heathen, whoſe diſtinguiſhed virtues are recorded, followed the example of their Gods, inſtead of being objects of our admiration and deſerved imitation, they would now be juſtly eſteemed by us as a reproach to human nature, and a diſgrace to every thing that was decent and laudable among men.

Inconceivable was the detriment, which the falſe Religion and ſhocking Superſtition of the *Greeks* and *Romans* did to the morals of the world. All their Gods are repreſented as inſtigated by envy, diſcord, revenge—by the worſt paſſions and moſt deteſtable vices, that can debaſe a frail

L 5 mortal.

mortal. No wonder, therefore, when their religious Syſtem itſelf breathed this ſpirit, that thoſe, who eſpouſed it as divine, as tranſmitted down to them from venerable and hoary Antiquity, ſhould imbibe it, and act from principle. It is natural to imitate the great Objects of our worſhip, in any qualities, which diſtinguiſhed them, and transfuſe into our ſpirits the ſame principles and diſpoſitions which actuated them. Their Religion was corrupt, their lives conſequently were corrupt.

This cannot be ſaid concerning our Divine Religion. It is a Syſtem of Holineſs and Charity, and the examples of thoſe, who founded it, are conſummate patterns of every diſtinguiſhed virtue it recommends. None can be betrayed into errours in conduct by copying too cloſely the great examples it exhibits for our imitation,

as

as the Heathens might be, and, alas !
often were. In the life of Jesus Christ
we see every fair and godlike virtue
shine, with which we are commanded
to adorn our own minds. He was a
most amiable and perfect pattern of
that meekness, benevolence, and charity his Gospel breathes. Exhorta-
tions to mutual affection, harmony,
and love, would come with infinite
force and energy from a person, who
displayed these before the world in all
their divine lustre by a most engaging
conversation. He, who was meek and
lowly in heart, who, when he was reviled, reviled not again, when he suffered, threatened not, who bore the
greatest indignities and abusive treatment with invincible meekness, and
a greatness of soul truly heroic and
unexampled, must assuredly give, by
the charms of such a personal conduct, a great additional force to virtues

tues which shone so conspicuous in his
own temper and affections.

He never can teach others Religion
and Morals with any success, whose
daily life contradicts his precepts.
He, who inculcates the duties of patience, and candour, and lenity, and
peaceableness, the government of our
passions, and the cultivation and improvement of every generous, humane, and benevolent disposition,
and yet whose life is known to be an
insult upon his instructions, is easily
provoked, is apt to kindle into violent outrageous passions, perhaps upon very trifling occasions, is petulant,
censorious, malicious, malevolent,
fond of scandal, and defamation, and
detraction, malignant in his temper,
and uncharitable in his reflections on
his fellow-men — what efficacy can
rules of duty have from such a character ?

It

It is not fo much what men fay, as how they live, that is the grand ob-ject of enquiry.   Now the blefled Re-ligion of Jefus will bear this fcrutiny. There is no defect in his life.   He exemplified every religious and mo-ral precept he enjoined upon others. His Religion, you know, is moft of all diftinguifhed for the duty of cha-rity and benevolence——and the life of Jefus was moft of all diftinguifhed for this divine virtue——for not only was the whole tenour of his life one uni-form feries of beneficence to the fouls and bodies of mankind, but his love for the world was ftronger than the love of life——for he voluntarily fur-rendered his life for the happinefs and falvation of the world.   Nay, fo un-conquered was his divine benevolence, that with his expiring breath he even prayed for his implacable, blood-thirfty murderers——making, in that moft affecting petition he addrefled to

God,

God, the only apology, which their aggravated crimes were capable of admitting : *Father, forgive them : for they know not what they do.*

As was the life and temper of Chrift, fo is the genius and fpirit of His Religion.   It has the peace of focieties and kingdoms, and the happinefs of families and individuals for its great object.   It labours to fecure this great end by exterminating from the human breaft all rancour, malice, bitternefs, and malignity—principles deftructive of all true happinefs, fubverfive of the true glory and dignity of our nature, and, whenever cherifhed, necefarily productive of public and private mifery and wretchednefs. This divine Religion, which defcended to us from the Father of lights, and bears the imprefs of the God of love, tends to make us like the God we ferve and the Redeemer we ac-

kinowknowledge, in purifying and sanctifying our natures, in rectifying our dispositions, in healing the moral disorders of our souls, and carrying us to the highest degrees of holiness and virtue we are capable of attaining. This Divine Religion engages us to look upon our fellow-creatures and fellow-Christians in the most endearing point of view——to make all candid, generous allowances for their frailties and imperfections——to do every thing in our power to alleviate their sorrows, mitigate their sufferings, and take off the pressure of human sorrows and calamities. This blessed Religion strives to extirpate from our bosom every root of bitterness, which, suffered to grow, might have a baneful influence both upon our own happiness and the happiness of those around us. The Religion of Jesus transforms men into a divine nature, exalts their views, dignifies and ennobles

bles their heaven-born spirits, mode-
rates and regulates the inferior affections, brings the animal paffions and
propenfities under a proper fubjection
and controul, fpreads a fcene of peace
and harmony and fatisfaction in the
foul, fills it with the kindeft affections
and focial benevolent difpofitions towards all, reftores the image of God,
which fenfual paffions had obfcured,
to its original luftre, and ftamps upon
it, in deep and indelible fignatures, that
wifdom that comes from above, that
is firft pure, then peaceable, gentle,
eafy to be entreated, full of mercy
and good fruits, without partiality,
and without hypocrify.

The Maker of our frame and the
Divine Jefus knew that the moft
pure, fublime, elegant, fubftantial,
and permanent happinefs, which man
could tafte on this fide heaven, would
refult from the mutual culture and

4   practice

practice of charity, love, beneficence, kindneſs, gentleneſs, meekneſs, candour, lenity, and univerſal good-will, — ſolely from a benevolent regard, therefore, to our own happineſs, he made theſe virtues the grand, fundamental indiſpenſable duties of his laſt and beſt diſpenſation to mankind—moſt mercifully, you ſee, connecting our intereſt with our duty, and our nobleſt happineſs with the nobleſt duty.

What a happy world ſhould we ſee, if Chriſtians lived but up to the rules of their common Religion! What harmony and concord would reign among different denominations and diſtinctions of Chriſtians, if their hearts and lives were but formed upon the charitable principles of the Goſpel of peace and love! What diſcords, and diſſentions, and animoſities, and uncharitable feuds and controverſies would now be unknown, had the

ſeveral

several parties of Chriſtians agreed to live up to our Lord's NEW COMMANDMENT—and comparatively diſregarding other things, as of an inferiour and ſubordinate ſignificancy and importance, had all ſhewed a virtuous and holy ſolicitude to tranſcribe into their hearts the true features of the Goſpel—to make their own perſonal conduct a ~~beautiful~~ Copy of the Divine Original—to exhibit before the world and one another, its divine form, to regulate their temper and diſpoſition by the laws it preſcribes— and had all been unanimouſly agreed, whatever their other differences might be, to be kindly-affectioned one towards another, forgiving one another, as God, for Chriſt's ſake, had freely forgiven them all. Happy world and happy age, in which the true ſpirit of the Goſpel ſhould revive with all its fair fruits and bleſſed effects—and all different Societies of Chriſtians

learn

learn to fpeak well and think favourably and candidly one of another.

This is what the Gofpel aims at—
this is what it is fitted in its nature to
produce—and the Scripture Prophecies clearly inform us, that thefe glorious and delectable fcenes in fome
fubfequent happy period it will produce. May God Almighty accelerate
thofe happy times, and by his over-
ruling Providence revive amongft us,
in the prefent age, more of the Chriftian Temper and Chriftian Spirit!

But let us not paffionately wifh and
antedate this happy æra of the Church
without doing every thing in our
power, in thofe feveral ftations and
fituations in which Providence hath
fixed us, to promote and advance it.
Let us fuffer the Gofpel to have its
full power upon our hearts and difpofitions—let us, according to our abilities

lities and capacities, read it carefully
with prayer to God, that we may
know it better, and practise it better——
let us imbibe its true spirit, which is
a spirit of love and charity——let our
benevolence be as boundless and unlimited as the creation of God——whatever we may err in, let us take care
not to err by cherishing a narrow,
contracted, censorious, uncharitable
disposition and spirit. Let the love
of God and of Christ, which shine
with such signal lustre in this dispen-
sation of grace and truth, inspire us
with love towards one another. Let
us banish every thing that is mean
and illiberal from our souls, as being
a disgrace to our natures, and a dis-
credit to our Religion ; and let us
make it our study and ambition, it is
a most noble and laudable ambition,
if it be possible, as much as lieth in
us, to live peaceably with all men.——
He who hath his passions under the
best

beſt government, is the happieſt man;
and he, who has a heart moſt inflamed with the love of God and Chriſt,
and mankind, who has the moſt charitable, benevolent affections, is the
beſt Chriſtian. He that is a true
Chriſtian, will ſhew to the world what
Chriſtianity is by his daily practice—
by doing all the good he can to thoſe
who are around him, of all parties
without diſtinction, will faithfully exhibit to the world in his own temper
and ſpirit what an amiable and divine ſyſtem the Goſpel is, when reduced to practice,⁺ how perfective of
human nature and human happineſs,
and will give the faireſt evidence of
its divine veracity and beneficial tendency, by the ſteady conſcientious
improvement of that fair train of virtues, which characterize it, which
eminently diſtinguiſh it above every
other religion the world ever ſaw, and
which will for ever conſtitute its conſummate

summate excellence and matchless glory and perfection. *The fruit of the
Spirit is love, joy, peace, long-suffering, gentleness, goodness, faith, meekness.* —

I will offer a few practical obser-
vations on these several particulars according to the order in which they
occur.

Amongst the blessed effects and
fruits, which the true spirit of the
Gospel produceth, the first, which
the Apostle mentions, is LOVE. *The
fruit of the Spirit is* LOVE. This is
the distinguishing glory of the Christian Religion, and consequently the
distinguishing glory of every Christian.

The professors of other religions
have been distinguished from the rest
of mankind by some discriminating tenets,

nets, or by some outward badges.
The Christian also was intended to
wear publickly and privately his characteristic mark, by which he was to
be universally known and contradis-
tinguished from the professors of all
other religions : *By this*, says our Saviour, *shall all men know that you are
my disciples, if you love one another.*
This was ever designed to be the
great test and peculiar characteristic
of a Christian. One of the early Fathers informs us, that nothing was
more common in the primitive ages
of the Church than for Heathens,
who were witnesses of that mutual
affection, harmony, and love, which
then reigned among Christians, to utter this exclamation : *See how the
Christians love one another !*

The spirit of the Gospel is not a
morose, reserved, narrow, illiberal,
uncharitable spirit. The Gospel is
an

an enemy to every-thing mean and contracted, abject and groveling. Its aim
is to exterminate from the heart every
ignoble paffion, every partial, ungene-
rous difpofition, and to expand it to its
utmost capacity with the principles of
univerfal benevolence and love. He,
who never felt the power and force
of thefe principles, never knew what
it was to be a Chriftian. He, who
is a ftranger to the influence of Charity and Love, is yet a ftranger to
every thing that is peculiarly evangelical. Let his abilities be what they
will—let his mental endowments, and
literary attainments be what they
will—let his acquifitions of hiftorical
and philofophical knowledge, the improvements he hath made in polite
learning, in modern arts and fciences,
or even in theological ftudies and refearches, be what they will—if he
have not, with all thefe fhining treafures of erudition and knowledge, a
chari-

charitable heart, he hath not the heart
of a Chriſtian—he is yet to learn what
it is to be a Chriſtian—what the Goſpel is—what is its genius and tendency—what it was deſigned to make
men—for what end it was that Chriſt
lived and died. For Chriſtianity is
entirely a practical inſtitution—entirely calculated by infinite Wiſdom
to mend the heart, to meliorate our
diſpoſitions, ſweeten our affections,
and to inſpire us with ſympathetic
pity, tenderneſs, and love one to another, in this common ſcene of human frailty, errour, and mortality.

One would think our common ſuf-
ferings in this vale of tears would
unite us one to another in the bonds
of one common Religion. One would
think a promiſcuous ſtate of undiſ-
tinguiſhed frailty, in which we are all
expoſed to ſo many ſorrows and mi-
ſeries—the common lot of humanity—

in

in which we are obnoxious to fo
many painful difeafes, fatal diftem-
pers, and unforeſeen cafualties and
difafters—in which we feel and are
deftined to feel the incumbent pref-
fure of fo many evils and fufferings,
which we can neither avert nor foften—
one would think, ftrangers and fo-
journers as we all are in a tranfitory
life—vulnerable, as we all are, every
moment, by the fhafts of death—
fellow-fufferers and fellow-travellers in
a world which is not our home—in
an imperfect, fugitive fcene of imperfect being—one would think thefe
common calamities would endear us
to each other, engage us, by focial
converfation and an intercourfe of
friendly offices, to alleviate the te-
dium of life's rugged road, and, by
a mutual endeavour to be as agreeable to each other as poffible, to fufpend and foften thofe miferies we cannot fhun. Humanity requires this—
                                    Chrif-

Chriftianity requires this. *Be kindly-affectioned one towards another. You yourfelves*, fays the Apoftle, *are taught of God to love one another.* God teaches this—Chrift teaches this—Nature teaches and prompts us to this, with all its generous powers and affections. *He that loveth not, knoweth not God; for God is love*, fays St. John. By the culture of this we have communion with God, who is pure benevolence—When under its generous, benign influence, the fame attributes govern us which actuate the Deity. This is the brighteft reflection of the Divine Image upon our fouls—this is the neareft and beft affimilation to the character of the bleffed God, who is good to all, who makes his fun to rife and his rain to fall upon juft and unjuft without diftinction. He who cherifhes the divine principle of benevolence participates the nature of God and the happinefs of God. The only

thing

thing we know of heaven is, that harmony, concord, benevolence and love reign amongſt all its bleſſed inhabitants—and he, who has his heart dilated with charity and love, begins his heaven here—for heaven is nothing more than the preſent ſtate carried on and afterwards compleated. Its commencement is in this world. Here we are to acquire ſuch diſpoſitions as are indiſpenſably requiſite to our future fruition of its bleſſedneſs—And theſe diſpoſitions, which we are commanded to cultivate and improve, give us, in their acquiſition and culture, a vigorous foretaſte and perception of that more perfect and conſummate felicity that awaits us in a happier ſtate of future being. He, therefore, who has the principle of love and benevolence in the greateſt perfection, diſplays the neareſt imitation of God, and the brighteſt aſſimilation to the joys of the bleſſed—for

this

this virtue yields the moſt refined, elegant, heart-ennobling felicity that the ſoul is capable of ſenſing.

Hence it appears how perfective of human nature and human happineſs the Goſpel is, which is founded in the love of God and the love of mankind, and which, by the injunction of charity as its capital article, engages us to live the life of God, to begin our heaven on earth, and to antedate the joys of glorified ſpirits. *He that loveth not his brother, whom he hath ſeen, how can he love God, whom he hath not ſeen? He that ſaith, he loveth God, and hateth his* Chriſtian *brother, is a liar*——all his pretenſions to the Chriſtian character are hypocritical and falſe. *This commandment have we from him, that he that loveth God, ſhould love his brother alſo.*

M 3　　　　　　All

All the privileges and bleſſings, with which the Goſpel Covenant hath inveſted us, are urged as ſo many incitements to mutual affection and Chriſtian love. All the diſtinguiſhing advantages, with which Chriſtians are bleſſed, are recounted and alledged as ſo many cogent arguments and motives to conciliate our affections one to another, to unite our hearts indiſſolubly one to another, and to induce them to coaleſce as one regular, harmonious ſociety, cemented by the ſtricteſt ties, and endeared to one another by the moſt tender and affecting bonds of union. *Beloved, if God ſo loved us, we ought to love one another.* That this is the primary deſign and ultimate end of the Goſpel inſtitution is apparent from every part and page of its ſyſtem. It univerſally repreſents charity and love as a compleat epitome and comprehenſive ſummary of the whole moral law. *He that loveth his*

his brother, hath fulfilled the law : love is the fulfilling of the law : if there be any other commandment, it is briefly comprehended in this, Thou shalt love thy neighbour as thyself. The end of the commandment, the Apostle means, the end of the Christian Law, *is charity, out of a pure heart, and of a good conscience, and of faith unfeigned.*

That Christian, therefore, who hath a good heart, and good dispositions to do good, who is in charity with all the world, who hath a heart too enlarged for the narrowness of party, and who embraces in the ample circle of its affections all mankind, this is a Christian——he hath the heart of a Christian——and shews what the true meaning and spirit of the New Testament is, better than all the Commentaries in the Vatican.

M 4 Suffer

Suffer me to suggest a few thoughts upon the next particular mentioned by the Apostle among the effects of Christianity. *The fruit of the Spirit is love,* joy——And who hath such cause of joy—equal pretensions to joy—as a good Christian ?——He, who is blessed with such privileges, endowed with such immunities, and invested with the fœderal character and distinguished title of *Sons of God* and *Heirs of God.* Can there be a happier being in the whole circle of the creation than a sincere Christian, who is conscious he is an object of the divine love, a subject of the mediatorial kingdom of Jesus, and not only an expectant, but an heir of immortality.

With what devout and sacred joy did the privileges of the Gospel inspire the Apostles in all the dreadful scenes of sorrow and persecution, with which they conflicted ? In all the
diffi-

difficulties and trials they suffered, their *rejoicing* was this, the testimony of a good conscience. They speak of themselves as sorrowful, yet always *rejoicing*. Among the duties they enjoin upon Christians, this was a distinguished one—a devout joy, a sacred exultation in the blessings and privileges of the Gospel. *Rejoice evermore*. There is nothing gloomy and melancholy in the Gospel—nothing to overwhelm us in pensive dejection and sullen despair. The Gospel is full of joy unspeakable, and comfort ineffable. It opens to its virtuous believer all the sources of the divinest joy. The Apostle exclaims in a flood of holy rapture, and in all the excesses of a most transporting joy : *Blessed be the God and Father of our Lord Jesus Christ, who hath loved us, and given us everlasting consolation.*

M 5   Those

Those are objects of my fincre pity, who can fee nothing chearful and delectable in the Gofpel: The Gofpel was given to fmooth and fweeten our paffage through this world—to fill us with joy and peace in believing—to foothe and fufpend the miferies of human life—to mitigate and alleviate the various difficulties and forrows we meet—and enable us to look, with filial confidence and joyful hope, to the God and Father of our Lord Jefus Chrift, affuring ourfelves, that he, who fpared not his Son, but delivered him up for us all, will alfo freely beftow every inferior bleffing.

Who, that confiders what immortality is, can indulge to chearlefs, defponding gloom and melancholy? How delightful is it, what a theme for facred joy, to have a world affured to us, in which we fhall exift for ever—in which our natures will be perfected—

perfected—and our happiness prove commensurate to its endless duration? What an inexhaustible subject of Christian joy is the prospect of glory, honour, and immortality!

APPLICATION.

Let these animating, these exhilarating truths, call forth all our sacred passions and devout affections. Let the privileges of the Gospel Covenant excite the most rapturous emotions, and awaken in our hearts the most pure and elegant sensibilities. Let us not affront and insult the good Being, who freely gave us this profusion of blessings, by a heart cold and languid and torpid and insensible—but let us entertain and cherish the quickest sense and most lively perception of them by *rejoicing* in that God who bestowed them—bestowed them to make us happy in the fruition

tion of them—and by indulging that
Chriſtian joy and chearfulneſs which
is ſo friendly to our nature and ſo
friendly to our Religion.　Let us
ſhew to the world, that the Goſpel
has produced in our hearts the happy
fruits of love, joy, peace, and tranquillity—and by cheriſhing in our bo-
ſoms theſe delightful principles here,
on earth, let us prepare for that bleſſed world, where the moſt triumphant
joy dwells and reigns for ever.

SERMON IX.

GAL. v. 22, 23.

The fruit of the Spirit is love, joy, peace, long-suffering, gentleness, goodness, faith, meekness, temperance: against such there is no law.

HAving shewn at large the nature of the Gospel, and the excellent fruits and blessed effects, of which it is productive—that its design.

sign is to rectify the human heart, to
regulate the affections, to inspire us
with the most generous benevolence—
by the culture and exercise of these
worthy dispositions manifestly tending to carry us to the highest degree
of moral perfection and happiness—
having proposed, in my discourse on
this subject, to expatiate on the several particular virtues here distinctly
enumerated as the genuine offspring
of the Gospel, and having already offered some practical remarks on the
two first mentioned—I now beg leave
to turn your reflections to a few
thoughts on another happy product
of the Christian spirit, and that is
PEACE. *The fruit of the Spirit is love,
joy,* PEACE.

The Gospel infuses into the mind
the truest peace, for it frees it from
the tyranny of turbulent passions, ex-
tinguishes the wild flames of irregular

ear, exorbitant affections, and com-
poses all its powers into harmony
and order. The principles of the
Christian Religion are the most sovereign and effectual antidote against
immoderate grief and sorrow—against
all anxious, tormenting fears—and
disconsolate, desponding thoughts.
The Religion of Jesus fills the heart
with divine tranquillity, with calm,
serene satisfaction—gives the human
mind the noblest possession of itself—
gives us the truest relish of our existence—makes every thing around us
wear a friendly and grateful aspect—
and exhibits human life, through its
medium, in the most pleasing and
agreeable colours, in the most amiable
point of view, as an inconsiderable,
minute part of one grand, stupendous
Whole, and as a scene introductory to
an everlasting duration.

The

The Gospel, you know, is by way
of diftinction called the *Gofpel of
Peace*—becaufe it imparts the moft
pure, facred, and permanent peace——
and is, in its nature, fitted to communicate to the mind the nobleft peace
and the nobleft happinefs. Muft
not that Religion infufe the moft
cheating, foothing fatisfaction into the foul, that enables us to look
up to the bleffed God with filial affection and with liberal confidence——
firmly perfuaded of his conftant guar-
dianfhip and protection of us and ours
—pleafingly affured that this good
Being will finally make all things
work together for our good, and that
our feveral ftations, conditions, and
circumftances in this fcene of being,
are his all-wife appointment. Muft it
not fill the mind with ferene tranquillity, compofure, and peace, to regard ourfelves under the fuperintend-
ence of infinite Power, Wifdom, and
Good.

Goodnefs—to confider the ever-bleffed God, as our moft indulgent and affectionate Parent, folicitous for our happinefs for both worlds, and regulating all the meafures of his government and the difpenfations of his Providence to us in this world in fuch a manner, as appears to his infinite wifdom beft calculated to promote our temporal welfare and everlafting felicity. To view God in Chrift as reconciling the world to himfelf, not imputing their trefpaffes to them—as defirous that none of his creatures fhould finally perifh, but be all happy in the fruition of himfelf and the enjoyment of endlefs happinefs—as freely offering to all the conditions and terms of falvation by Jefus Chrift—and taking every method, but what is inconfiftent with the law of our nature and the liberty of human actions, to engage them to comply with thefe conditions — to confider
the

the blessed God, from a principle of compassion and benevolence for the human race, sending his Son to redeem the world, *that every one that believeth in him should not perish, but have everlasting life*——what sacred pleasure and sacred peace do these grateful, pleasing thoughts instil into all our rational and intellectual powers ——how happy do they make us in our existence, conscious of the love and friendship of the God and Father of our Lord Jesus Christ——conscious that we are the objects of his love, and that our best interests for time and eternity are his care.

These evangelical truths shed their selectest influence over human life—— they shed their selectest influence over every human bosom, infusing joy and peace and consolation *unspeakable and full of glory.* The conscious sense of the pardon of my past sins

upon

upon fincere repentance and genuine remorfe—the confcious fenfe that my happinefs is the care of God—that myfelf and all my concerns are in the hands of a faithful Creator, who will never defert me, who formed me for immortality, and will as affuredly beftow it as he hath promifed it — a deep, affecting, penetrating, confcious fenfe of thefe TRUTHS, fmooths our fhort paffage through this life — makes us pleafed with ourfelves and every thing around us—fpreads the moft delectable profpects before us— converts this wildernefs into a paradife—converts apparent irregularity, diforder, and confufion, into a delightful, tranfporting fcene of beauty, harmony, and order.

What can invade the peace of that mind, that is under the influence of thefe truths? *If God is for us*, fays the Apoftle, fpeaking on this very fubject,

ject, *who can be against us?* If we have peace of conscience, and the approbation of our Maker, no evil can hurt us. We read of a PEACE, *which the world can neither give, nor take away.* This is that *peace* which the principles of the Gospel inspire. It is called, elsewhere, *the* PEACE *of God, which passeth all understanding*—that is—such a mental happiness, such pure, sacred, divine, heart-ennobling satisfactions flow from this *peace of God,* as surpass all the most enlarged ideas, and transcend all the most elevated conceptions of the human mind.

Almost the last words our blessed Saviour addressed to his disconsolate Disciples were these: *My* PEACE *I give you, my* PEACE *I leave unto you: not as the world giveth*—Alas: the *peace* and happiness which result from worldly acquisitions are liable to many cruel interruptions—continually lie at the mercy

mercy of ten thousand accidents and
disasters—will not support us in an
hour of pain and distress—much less
in the hour of death. But that peace
of mind, which is the *fruit of the spi-*
rit of the Gospel, is founded on a basis
which nothing can subvert—is esta-
blished on a rock, which the storms
of life's tempestuous ocean assail in
vain—it is a peace that is liable to no
interruptions from things external—
it fluctuates not with every fluctuating
scene—it is a peace, which continues
with us, chearing and consoling us
when every thing else hath abandoned
us—and, what enhances and endears
this divine peace most to us is, that
it throws out the most consolations
and supports in an hour of sorrow,
and in the article of death. For he,
who hath this peace of mind, a peace,
arising from a sense of the complacential favour of God, and the applaud-
ing testimony of a good conscience, is
enabled

enabled to support all the trials of this world with heroic firmnefs and Chriftian magnanimity, to leave the world without regret, without a figh; and to meet death with ferene compofure, with undaunted fortitude, as being only an introduction to the happy regions of eternal peace. *Mark the perfect man, and behold the upright; for the end of that man is* PEACE.

Thus it appears, that the Gofpel is calculated to impart to us the trueft PEACE of mind——that PEACE is one of the happy fruits of this amiable fpirit——and that its principles, doctrines, and promifes have the nobleft tendency to infpire us with *joy and* PEACE *in believing.*

I proceed to offer a few remarks in the next particular mentioned in the text; which is LONG-SUFFERING. *The fruit of the Spirit is love, joy, peace,*

LONG-

LONG-SUFFERING. This relates to the proper government of our spirits, and the virtuous difcipline, in which we ought to have our minds—not burfting into a wild flame of paffion with every provocation that is offered us: not inftantly kindling into rage and fury with every mean fpark that happens to light upon us. Self-government is one of the moft ufeful leffons we can learn. He, who hath not his paffions under proper regulation—he, who hath not power over his own fpirit, is liable to have his peace of mind violated, and his happinefs difturbed and broken, by every trifling infult, which is unavoidable in this world. Calumny, abufe, and ill treatment, we cannot efcape—we live in a cenforious, malevolent world—the greateft integrity and innocence are not fafe—the beft Chriftian is not privileged from the fhafts of malice and detraction—and the more confcien-

tious

tious and upright, consequently the
more singular, and consequently the
more aspersed and scurrilized——Amidst
these scenes, what is our conduct,
what is our support, what temper and
disposition does the Gospel require——
O blessed, celestial system ! O sacred,
divine volume ! it teaches this heavenly lesson.: *Love your enemies ; bless
them that curse you : do good to them
that hate you, and pray for them who
despitefully use you and persecute you.*

The Gospel was intended to curb
our exorbitant passions, to restrain
and moderate our animal propensities,
and to bring them in subjection to the
law of reason and of God. Neither
the principles nor the examples of the
Gospel justify a retaliation of injuries,
and our returning abusive treatment
with any malignant recriminations.
The reverse it insists upon as our duty
——to retaliate injuries with kindness,

I   to

to return evil with good, to requite abuse with blessing, and malice with prayer. Blessed Religion! which conspires to make a paradise in our bosoms, to transform human nature into divine, to exalt us above the reach of sublunary evils, and to ally us to angels and happy spirits in the temper and disposition of our minds.

What conduct does the Gospel enjoin us to observe towards those, who are instigated by implacable resentment against us? Hear the words of the Apostle: *If thy enemy hunger, feed him; if he thirst, give him drink: for in so doing thou shalt heap coals of fire upon his head.* This is the true spirit of the Gospel, which it is your duty and mine to acquire—to *put on, as the elect of God, bowels of mercies, kindness, humbleness of mind, meekness, long-suffering; forbearing one another, if any man have a quarrel against*

N

any,

any, even as Chrift forgave you, fo alfo do ye.

The example of Chrift is here propofed as a model for our imitation—and what an affecting, endearing pattern hath he exhibited in his conduct! He was brought, you know, as a lamb to the flaughter; and as a fheep before his fhearers is dumb, fo he opened not his mouth. Who endured the contradiction of finners againft himfelf—who, when he was reviled, reviled not again; when he fuffered, he threatened not, but committed himfelf to him who judges righteoufly.

Let us think of this divine Example in fimilar circumftances, and act as our Divine Mafter did under injurious treatment and unprovoked abufe. Take my yoke upon you, and learn of me; for I am MEEK.

One

One would think such an example as this might check and for ever suppress all our rising resentments, would disarm rage and passion, and make all our worst affections subside into Christian meekness, lenity, and long-suffering. Shall I suffer my passions to be inflamed with every petty injury, when my Saviour calmly endured the greatest?——Shall I suffer my resentment to kindle into a wild furious flame at this real or supposed provocation, when my Saviour patiently supported the last indignities?——How unlike shall I render myself to my blessed Redeemer, if, when I am reviled, I revile again; if when I suffer, I threaten; and return every abuse and injury with an acrimony, virulence, and temper, O how unworthy a disciple of the meek and lowly Jesus!

Our Religion hath taught us nothing, if it have not taught us the

govern-

government of our paſſions. He hath little pretenſions to the Chriſtian ſpirit, who can load the objects of his reſentment with odious names and ſcurrilous expreſſions. This is a language no Chriſtian ever learned in the ſchool of Jeſus. *The wrath of man worketh not the righteouſneſs of God,* or the promotion of truth. He is to learn what it is to be a Chriſtian, who is yet to learn patience and peaceableneſs. An inflammable ſpirit, an unforgiving temper—what a contraſt this to the temper and ſpirit of the inoffenſive Jeſus! What a wretched and miſerable creature is he, who is the ſport of every paſſion—who is continually moroſe, fretful, irritable —hath a heart perpetually gnawed and corroded by the dæmon of paſſion and peeviſhneſs—who pours the overflowings of his own infelicity upon every object around him—who is inceſſantly tormented with inward inquietude

quietude——diſtracted by the tumul-
tuous conflict of a thouſand raging
and contending paſſions——loving no
one, beloved by no one——all perſons
cautiouſly ſhunning and avoiding
him, left they ſhould inadvertently
happen to ſay or do ſomething that
might kindle his paſſions into a flame.

One cannot conceive of a more
compleatly wretched being than he
who is tyrannized over by his paſſions, and whoſe whole ſoul is under
the abſolute dominion of malice, diſcord, pride, and reſentment. The
Goſpel, therefore, ſtudies and con-
ſults human happineſs by reſtoring
the mind to itſelf, by repreſſing this
lawleſs diſorder, quelling this tu-
multuous uproar, and poſſeſſing it
with calm compoſure and unruffled
tranquillity. Well-governed paſſions,
well-diſciplined, regulated affections, a
ſerene mind, a calm, undiſturbed bo-

fom—thefe are the bleffed effects of
the Chriftian fpirit, where Chriftianity
is cordially imbibed, affiduoufly cultivated, and diligently exercifed and
improved. The principles of the
Gofpel will enable us to fuftain reproachful treatment with invincible
compofure, to fupport abufe and calumny without any querulous invec-
tives and bitter recriminations, to
bear our forrows without any mur-
muring words or repining expreffions, to requite evil with good,
and with placid refignation to fubmit
ourfelves to that God, who will one
day judge between us.

GENTLENESS is the next virtue that
occurs in this diftinct enumeration of
the various bleffed fruits of the Spirit. *Gentlenefs* denotes a mild, meek,
modeft, difpaffionate frame of mind—
a prudent, cautious temper, ever afraid
of giving unneceffary offence. Such a
temper

temper is extremely worthy a Chriſtian, and above all, a Chriſtian Miniſter. A fear of diſpleaſing by any thing unguarded—a cautious, virtuous timidity of diſguſting mens' paſſions without cauſe—an amiable attainment this — a moſt lovely and Chriſtian endowment this ; highly ornamental of our nature, highly ornamental of the Goſpel. To converſe with perſons of different tempers and various diſpoſitions, and yet pleaſe—pleaſe, but not at the expence of either truth or conſcience — pleaſe, merely by a prudent, diffident, humble, offencelefs carriage—is no vulgar acquiſition.

It requires great care, great prudence, great diſcipline, to be maſter of ourſelves on all occaſions—to acquire the knowledge of ourſelves : it is the moſt uſeful of all kinds of knowledge, and to maintain our ſpi-

rit

rit under an equal, regular fubjection and government. I never knew a
perfon, and believe I never fhall know
any one, that was ever convinced by
fupercilious airs, by dogmatical affertions, by contemptuous expreffions,
by banter and derifion, and treating
an opponent with fovereign difre-
fpect, by pronouncing the emphatical
words, *abfurd* and *ridiculous*, in a dif-
dainful manner. I do not know how
others are affected—but I own I always diftruft thofe arguments, and
fufpect that caufe that is forced upon
me by imperious, pofitive affertions,
and obtruded upon my underftanding
and reafon by the dint of clamour, af-
furance, and compulfion. Truth is a
calm, cool, difpaffionate thing, and
requires not any thing boifterous and
oftentatious to make it appear to advantage. Mildnefs and gentlenefs are
the moft pleafing vehicles, in which
to convey it to the underftanding and
heart.

heart.   Modesty greatly prepossesseth us in favour of any principles it diffidently recommends.   Modesty and diffidence are powerful enough to prejudice us in favour even of principles that are erroneous and fallacious.   I am sure that he, who maintains a temper calm, mild, unruffled, is in the best frame for the investigation of truth, and hath vastly the advantage of an adversary in any debate and disquisition.

There is hardly any virtue so frequently recommended to Ministers of the Gospel, as this amiable temper of mind.   *Be wise as serpents, and harmless as doves.   Let your moderation be known to all men.   The servant of the Lord must not strive, but be gentle towards all men : in meekness instructing those who oppose themselves.*   The greatest infelicity a Minister can labour under with regard to the advancement

N 5   of

of truth and fecuring the ends of his miniftry, is a violent temper. Violence is like pride——it always defeats itfelf.

It is a lamentable confideration to think, how many learned perfons never learned the art of governing their paffions. He is very unfit to be an inftructor of others in morals, who is yet to learn one of the principal branches of Ethicks, I mean, felf-knowledge, felf-government. With what force and fuccefs can precepts and directions to meeknefs, gentlenefs, moderation, candour, diffidence, prudence, difcretion, inoffenfivenefs, come from a perfon, who is known to be eafily tranfported into paffion upon frivolous pretences, to be morofe, proud, arrogant, fupercilious, refentful, of an implacable, haughty, arbitrary, unforgiving fpirit. Sweetnefs of difpofition, uniformity of temper, mild-

mildnefs of carriage, a fpirit calm, ferene, tranquil, not irritable by trifles, not ruffled, as fome unhappy, felf-tormenting tempers are, even by the moft diftant appearance of an infult, is a moft engaging, amiable ornament to every Chriftian and to every Minifter.

If there was any virtue, that predominated in our Lord's character, it was his MEEKNESS. All the provocations he met with never extorted from him a fingle unguarded expreffion. One would think his harmlefs inoffenfivenefs would have difarmed their rage, and converted the tongue of malice and detraction into admiration and praife. His gentle, placid, placable fpirit forgave them, and prayed that God would forgive them—— His conduct towards his Difciples is very obfervable, and highly worthy our imitation. Though he poffeffed all

all the treasures of wisdom and knowledge, yet what kind, generous allowances did he make for their Jewish
errours and prejudices—how compaf-
fionately candid was he to their imperfections, not difclofing the whole
fyftem of heavenly truths all at once,
but communicating them gradually,
as their minds were capable of bear-
ing them—removing their former errours by gentle, infenfible degrees—
imparting his divine doctrines in larger and larger meafures as their powers
enlarged—not offending them, not
difgufting them by any harfh, unfea-
fonable truths, by any pofitive over-
awing, defpotic affertions, but infinu-
ating his facred inftruction into their
minds by every engaging, endearing
method, that could win their affections and attract their love. Bleffed
pattern for us to copy ! He is the beft
Chriftian, who attains the neareft refemblance to it. It was his character,
a noble

a noble and divine character it is. God
grant we may make it the worthy object of our imitation, That *he was holy
and* HARMLESS.

Of the next virtues, GOODNESS,
FAITH, MEEKNESS, the first denotes
goodnefs of heart——a heart difpofed to
do good——full of love of God and love
to man——a kind, benevolent difpofition, prompt to relieve indigence and
penury, and to make all happy around
it. Such a heart and fuch a difpofition are particularly the *fruit of the
Spirit* —— the offspring of the Gofpel,
which is wholly a fcheme of benevolence, a fyftem of univerfal charity,
love, and goodnefs.

Our Saviour fpeaks of a *good tree
bringing forth good fruit,* and of the
treafures of a good heart. A beneficent
heart, whofe affections breathe univerfal benevolence, whofe difpofitions

are

are replete with kindnefs, fympathy, pity, and compaffion, is truly evangelical—is fuch a heart as the Gofpel requires, and its principles produce. A heart full of charity and goodnefs bears the faireft impreffion of the Divinity, whofe favourite Attribute is infinite Goodnefs—bears the neareft, happieft refemblance to the humane and benevolent Jefus, whofe character it is—that he went about continually doing good.

The *fecond* of thefe, which we tranflate *faith*, ought to have been rendered *fidelity*. It denotes a punctual, confcientious fidelity in our words and actions—faithfulnefs to our promifes: —a fcrupulous juftice and honour in our dealings—and a ftrict, inviolable probity and integrity in the whole of our conduct. He, that falfifies his word, forfeits his character—he, that violates his promife and betrays his truft, truſt, weakens his reputation, loſes his credit, and renders himſelf an ob- ject of contempt.

One of the moſt amiable characters I ever remember to have met with in the whole courſe of my reading, is that given by our bleſſed Saviour to Nathanael—*Behold an Iſraelite indeed, in whom there is no guile*—that is, a man of ſtrict probity, of conſcientious integrity. Sincerity is a moſt ami- able virtue, and commands univerſal love. Every other good quality, eve- ry other virtuous attainment, without ſincerity, ſeparate from ſincerity, is a worthleſs, uſeleſs acquiſition. Since- rity of heart, ſimplicity of life—how lovely are theſe both in the ſight of God and man!——What ornaments are they of human nature and of the Goſpel! If our Religion have not produced ſincerity, it hath produced nothing of any avail to our final ſalva- tion.

tion. God requires the heart. *My son, give me thy heart.* If this be not devoted to God and holiness, no other sacrifice we can offer in lieu of it will be accepted. We cannot elude the Divine inspection. Hypocrisy will be of no avail to us. We cannot impose upon the great Spectator of our hearts by any specious artful dissimulation. *Be not deceived, God is not mocked.* He, who can make an appeal to the great God with the Apostle, that in *simplicity and godly sincerity he hath had his conversation in the world,* may look up to heaven with confidence. One of the characters given of God in the Scriptures is, that he is *true and faithful, and cannot lie. God, who cannot lie.* How greatly then, let the hypocrite tremble, how greatly must falshood, and artifice, and dissimulation, and insincerity, be the detestation and abhorrence of that Being, who is truth and veracity itself! How unlike is he

to

to God, who is unfaithful to his promises, and insincere in his professions!
Let the divine Spirit of our divine
Religion then produce this blessed
fruit in us, to make us act at all
times from principles of integrity and
probity, and to render us conscien-
tiously upright and sincere in all our
dealings and transactions with the
world.

Meekness hath been sufficiently
explained and urged under some
of its kindred virtues here enumerated.

I proceed therefore to the last particular in the Apostle's minute de-
scription of the *fruits of the Spirit.*
Temperance closes this fair and
splendid list—and amidst these resplendent jewels of the Christian's
crown shines with distinguished lustre.

I know

I know of no virtue productive of happier consequences than TEMPERANCE. Both the *body* and *mind* eminently share the benign effects of this most salutary virtue. The *mind* of a temperate man is always alert, chearful, and vigorous—free in its intellectual operations—in the true possession of itself—at perfect liberty for concerting and executing any measures — unimpeded, unembarrassed with any obstacles from impure, unsatiated appetites — is the happiest frame for acquiring knowledge, for exploring truth, and for pursuing any thing that can enhance the dignity, honour, reputation, and happiness of our natures.

The *body* too signally participates the happy consequences of this excellent virtue. It enables all the parts to perform their respective functions with liberty, freedom, and expedition

tion——prevents that fatal train of difeafes occafioned by intemperance and voluptuoufnefs——prevents the ravages of that deftructive monfter which hath flain more of the human race than ever the fword did. An ancient writer informs us, that during that dreadful plague, which almoft unpeopled *Athens*, in the firft year of the *Peloponnefian* war, and by which feveral thoufands were cut off, *Socrates* enjoyed uninterrupted health ; and the writers, fays he, who mention this incident, afcribe the Philofopher's prefervation folely to his temperance.

How many have deftroyed their health, and for ever ruined their conftitutions, by intemperance——fuffering in the flower and prime of life all the miferies of old age? You and I can alledge many unhappy inftances. *The wages of fin is* untimely *death*——and above all fins the wages of intemperance

rance is death. Young men need not, they cannot have, a stronger motive to sobriety and virtue, than the sight of those many miserable and shocking spectacles, who have reduced themselves to this wretched condition by the vicious courses they pursued. We have ten thousand living proofs to convince us, were we disposed to learn that wisdom they read us, that it is for no man's interest to overleap the bounds of temperance. He, who once wilfully transgresses them, knows not to what lengths he may proceed——knows not where his career may stop, if by the grace of God his vicious career ever stop at all on this side eternity. It is very useful advice which our blessed Saviour gives us; would to God we ever kept it impressed on our hearts. *Take heed, lest at any time your hearts should be overcharged with surfeiting and drunkenness, and so that day should come upon you unawares.*

Dread-

Dreadful beyond defcription for a bad man to be cut off in a fit of intemperance, as thoufands have been, and in this condition to be fummoned before the tribunal of their Judge.

It is commonly faid, that profane fwearing is the only fin that hath no temptation to it, either from worldly profit or fenfual pleafure. Really I cannot fee what temptation there is for a man to put a force, a violence upon his nature, and ftupefy and deluge himfelf in a flood of intemperance. The brutes do not this. They fatisfy their cravings within the law of their natures, and the ftandard and meafure of their defires. Man is the only being, who without any temptation does injury to reluctant Nature—forces it involuntarily into a compliance, and degrades himfelf far below the brutes that perifh—And what is the confequence, the natural, necef-

neceffary confequence—The violation of the laws of our being is the bane and ruin of our being—all fuch violations impair the health, undermine the conftitution, and cut fhort the thread of life, long, long before it hath attained its full maturity—long before it hath reached that period which God affigned as the ultimate limits of mortal duration.

By the injunction of temperance, therefore, our Religion hath confulted the true welfare and happinefs of our natures, and contributes to render life a real bleffing to us. It cautions us againft thofe *flefhly lufts that war againft the foul,* at the fame time that they ruin and deftroy the body—and afferts that *our bodies are the temples of the Holy Ghoft,* and confequently that they ought to be confecrated to purity, fanctity, and temperance.

After

After diftinctly recounting thefe Chriftian virtues, *the fruits of the Spirit*, the Apoftle obferves, that *againft fuch there is no law*—that is—all law is founded upon them. All the laws, that ever were enacted in every age and nation enjoin thefe virtues, and ftamp their intrinfic excellence and worth by their authority and fanction. There never was any body of laws compiled by any legiflator in any country, that prefcribed duties contrary to thefe—the reverfe of thefe. Thefe virtues have a natural, inherent amiablenefs in them, and have been approved by all the wife and good that ever lived. All divine and human laws are erected upon thefe as their bafis, and eftablifh them as perfective of the true honour, dignity, and happinefs of human-kind. The Chriftian Law, by ratifying thefe virtues by its authoritative fanction, and enforcing the obfervance of them by

2

the

the moſt cogent motives and animating incentives, hath approved itſelf to be the perfection of all Religion, a Scheme, worthy the infinite goodneſs of God to communicate, and worthy the reception of ſuch beings as mankind. How often are we exhorted to give all diligence to add to our faith, virtue, knowledge, temperance, piety, brotherly love, charity—to adorn the Doctrine of God our Saviour by a life of univerſal Holineſs, and to make the genuineneſs of our faith in Jeſus Chriſt ſhine forth in an amiable life and converſation.

The moſt uſeful ſyſtem of morals, that ever was publiſhed to the world, is the New Teſtament. All the virtues, that can adorn our natures, fit us for the acceptance of God, and the future enjoyment of heaven, are there recommended, and urged upon its profeſſors by the moſt coercive and

affect-

affecting confiderations. The Gofpel
was defigned to carry our virtue and
holinefs to the higheft pitch of perfection, to the higheft, nobleft improvement that human nature can attain—
and if the Gofpel will not make us
holy, it were better for us if we had
never known it.

APPLICATION.

Let us then review our paft lives,
explore our hearts, and examine ourfelves by the plain rules and directions it lays down. What progrefs
have I made in holinefs—What good
have I done—What effect hath the
Gofpel produced in my heart and upon my difpofitions—Hath it made me
more like God in his purity and holinefs, more like my Redeemer in his
meeknefs, patience, piety, and peace-
ablenefs—Hath it transformed my
foul from the love and practice of fin

O

to

to the love and practice of goodness——
Have I that spirit and temper the
Gospel requires——Do its blessed fruits
adorn my daily life, and shine forth
in my conversation before my family
and the world——Or have I, as yet, an
heart insensible of the value of the
Gospel——Do I seldom, or but transi-
ently, think of my privileges and
blessings as a Christian——Am I negligent and careless about *walking so as
to please God*, and fulfil my Christian
duties——Is my heart affected and influenced, when I read the great things
my Redeemer hath done for me——Do
I make his directions the rule of my
life——Am I solicitous to embellish the
Christian life with these blessed *fruits
of the Sperit*, with *love*, *joy*, *peace*,
long-suffering, *meekness*, *temperance*——
How far have I answered the distinguishing character of a Christian in
doing works of charity, and admini-
stering

ftering relief to real objects of compassion?

These are useful enquiries—should be often repeated—should be fixed upon the mind by serious meditation—and the most deliberate resolutions should be formed in consequence of them. Did we habituate ourselves to this useful duty, SELF-EXAMINATION, in our moments of retirement, we should know our hearts better, make a greater progress than we do in the divine life, be more upon our guard against temptations, be more careful to please God and to adorn the Christian Profession.

May God endow us with the Christian Spirit, and enable us to bring forth its blessed fruits! May he grant of his infinite mercy, through Jesus Christ our Lord, that after we have conducted this mortal life in a manner

O 2 · worthy

worthy the vocation wherewith we are
called, we may be introduced into that
blessed world, where human frailty and
mortal imperfections are unknown,
and where perfect holiness and perfect
happiness reign triumphant for ever.

THE

THE

SPIRIT of CHRISTIANITY.

SERMON X.

LUKE ix. 55.

But he turned and rebuked them, and said, Ye know not what manner of spirit ye are of.

IF you confult the context, you will find the incident which gave occafion to the remarkable paffage I have read to you. Our Lord, intending to vifit Jerufalem, defpatched a number of perfons before him on the road to provide the neceſſary accommodations, as was uſual in thoſe days, when there were no inns and houſes of public entertainment for travellers. Theſe meſſengers accordingly entered a village belonging to the Samaritans —intending here to prepare what was proper againſt our Saviour's arrival. Between the Samaritans and Jews there ever ſubſiſted the moſt implacable enmity. The Jews could never forgive the Samaritans for deſerting the Temple Worſhip, and erecting a ſeparate Church on Mount Gerizim. And the Samaritans, as is uſual with all religious controverſialiſts, cheriſhed the blackeſt hatred and deadly animoſity againſt the Jews for building their Temple on Mount Moriah, contrary, as they imagined, to the divine preſcription. Differences about theſe frivolous and ridiculous trifles were kindled by their mutual diſcords to ſuch a flame, and had

tranſ-

tranſported, as, alas! is cuſtomary,
the diſputants on both ſides, to ſuch
dreadful uncharitableneſs, as to diſſolve all the mutual ties of humanity,
break all the bands of friendſhip and
ſociety between the two nations, and
totally extinguiſh, in the boſom of
both parties, every ſpark of affection,
kindneſs, and love for one another.
On account of theſe religious differences they carried their reſentment
againſt each other to ſuch deplorable
lengths, that they at laſt mutually
agreed only in this, to do one another
all the ill offices in their power, to
ſeize every opportunity to injure one
another's perſons and properties, to
load each other with the moſt odious
and reproachful names their malice
could invent, and to break off all
friendly intercourſe one with another.

Hence it was that the woman of
Samaria was aſtoniſhed that our Saviour,

viour, being a Jew, fhould fo far de-
part from the national pride, fhould
fo far forget the national antipathy,
as to folicit even fo trivial a favour as
a cup of cold water to flake his thirft
—for, as one of the Commentators
upon this paffage obferves, a Jew
would infinitely rather die with thirft,
than receive his life from the hand of
a Samaritan.

When the Jews were exafperated
beyond all bounds at our bleffed Saviour, the bittereft name their rage
launched againft him was, SAMARI-
TAN—*Thou art a* SAMARITAN, *and
haft a devil*—and even now a Samaritan is the firft odious term that a modern Jew's refentment dictates.

Our Saviour's meffengers entering
into a village belonging to this people, its inhabitants denied their Mafter the common rites of hofpitality,
and

and peremptorily refufed to admit him into the place. The reafon of this unufual and unheard-of refufal in a nation and age, where the rites of hofpitality were univerfally accounted fo facred and inviolable, appears from the words immediately following—— They denied him admiffion into the town, merely becaufe *his face was fet towards* JERUSALEM——becaufe his defign apparently was not to worfhip in *their* Temple, but in Jerufalem—— merely to pafs fwiftly through their territories without giving a fanction to their Temple, and recommending their national worfhip by his prophetic authority. This they deemed an unpardonable infult from one, who affumed a divine character; and took this imaginary-infult fo heinoufly, as publickly to refufe him that hofpitality, which in thofe times was never refufed.

Two

Two of his difciples, James and John, fired with indignation at this moft outrageous and difrefpectful treatment of their Mafter, inftantly flew to Jefus, and glowing with virulence and rage at the indignity offered him, immediately thus accofted him —Will you, Sir, give us leave to deftroy thefe inhofpitable wretches with fire from heaven, as Elias did his enemies?—

In this fanguinary requeft all the *Jew* appears. Nothing but torrents of fire, miraculoufly called from the fkies, would glut a *Jew's* revenge. You fee, from this fignal inftance, how the difciples of our Lord were actuated by Jewifh principles—how they were infligated by that perfecuting fpirit, which nothing will fatiate but the blood of the delinquent. You have here a ftriking proof, to what lengths the rage of perfecution will

tranftransport men, to the utter extinction of all humanity—that superstitious zeal and bigotry is an unfeeling thing —and that those, who are under the unhappy influence of religious rage and frenzy hesitate not, scruple not to satisfy their inflamed passions with the destruction of those, who have provoked their indignation.

Blessed God! what, the disciples of the meek and holy Jesus call for fire from heaven to consume *their* adversaries, as some of the Jewish prophets did *theirs!*——Was it possible, was it indeed possible that such unhallowed passions could dwell in bosoms, which had been so long under the influence of the heavenly instructions of the benevolent Jesus! Anger, says the poet, is a temporary madness. Anger overleaps all the bounds of common decency and common humanity——especially anger that is kindled,

I am

I am forry to remark it, from religious difputes.

One cannot but exprefs one's furprife at fuch a requeft, when we confider the *charaEter of the perfons* who made it——JAMES and JOHN——*James*, that excellent, amiable Apoftle, who has left us fuch a divine Epiftle, full of fuch ufeful inftructions, breathing in every line of it a temper and fpirit very different from what its author difcovered on this occafion —— The other perfon, who was for deftroying a number of his fellow-creatures by fire from heaven, aftonifhing to reflect, aftonifhing to reflect, was that Difciple, whom Jefus loved, whom he diftinguifhed above all the other Apoftles with particular, endearing marks of his affection and friendfhip, who leaned on his bofom, and who is no lefs than four times characterized by that *difciple whom Jefus loved.* The person,

person, who was for consigning to dire destruction the unhappy objects of his anger, was the Apostle JOHN, whose writings are replete with love, are embalmed with love, if I may use the expression, and discover a tenderness of Christian affection, and a diffusion of benevolence and charity, which infinitely endear his temper and disposition to every one who peruses them.

But the Disciples were now, alas! in a great measure strangers to the genius and spirit of our Saviour's Religion. They had all their Jewish prejudices and prepossessions about them, which our Lord chose to remove, not abruptly, nor precipitately, but with a gentle, lenient hand, in a gradual, insensible manner. Even after our Saviour's Resurrection it apappears, that the Apostles knew so little of the true nature of the Christian

tian Difpenfation, that they even then imagined, with the bulk of the Jewifh nation, that it was to be a temporal monarchy. The queftion they then addreffed to him was this: *Lord, wilt thou at this time reftore the kingdom to Ifrael?*——Wilt thou now, fince thou haft miraculoufly burft the barriers of the grave, erect a grand, magnificent empire, refcue thy native country from the fervitude of the Romans, and make Jerufalem the proud feat and center of a vaft, opulent, and invincible kingdom?

This inquifitorial requeft therefore of thefe two Difciples to wreak their vengeance on thefe poor deluded villagers proceeded from a Jewifh, not a Chriftian fpirit——proceeded from a deplorable ignorance of the genius of that Religion, in which their Divine Mafter came from heaven to inftruct men. One may look upon this inftance

ſtance before us as the firſt *beginning of perſecution* in the Chriſtian Church —as the date and commencement of all thoſe bloody ſcenes, with which the pages of Eccleſiaſtical Hiſtory are ſo diſgracefully polluted. Here is the *firſt inſtance* on record of the followers of Jeſus intimating an ardent deſire that even gracious heaven would interfere to extirpate, and by a miraculous infliction to conſume the objects of their worſt paſſions. And this ever-memorable paſſage ought to be an ever-memorable leſſon to all future ages, how averſe our bleſſed Redeemer was to perſecution, with what deteſtation and horror he regarded every attempt to hurt the perſons of men from a motive of injudicious, miſtaken zeal, and how infinitely contrary and repugnant he deemed a furious, uncharitable ſpirit to be to that temper and ſpirit, with which his Religion
gion

gion was primarily defigned to infpire all its profeffors.

Why was this paffage in our Saviour's hiftory recorded by the infpired hiftorian ?——Undoubtedly to read the Chriftian Church, in every age and nation of the world, a leffon of ufeful inftruction——that it was never the defign of our Lord, that errors in Religion fhould be confuted by fhowers of fire rained from heaven, or by the fword of the civil magiftrate ——that different parties and denominations of Chriftians fhould not be inftigated againft each other by uncharitable feuds and malignant difcords, but be ever difpofed to tolerate one another, forgive one another, if any one have a quarrel againft any, and to maintain the unity of the Spirit in the bond of Chriftian peace, concord, and love.

Our

Our Saviour, upon hearing expressions breathing such cruelty and revenge, turned to the persons from whom they proceeded, in the last amazement, astonished at such a public request from the public Preachers of his Religion. He then severely reproved them for such a rash, wicked, intemperate petition——He solemnly rebuked them for the cruel persecuting spirit they discovered on this occasion, and concluded with saying, YE KNOW NOT WHAT MANNER OF SPIRIT YE ARE OF. ——A sentence that deserves to be written in letters of gold on the walls of the Vatican——A sentence, that deserves to be written in letters of gold on the doors of every Inquisition in Europe——A sentence, that deserves to be written in the fairest characters in the study of every Christian Minister who is fond of temporal power——and, permit me to add, a sentence, that deserves to be written in indelible cha-

racters

racters on the heart of every Chriftian. *Ye know not what manner of fpirit ye are of*—You are unhappy ftrangers to the real temper, genius, and fpirit of my Gofpel.   You are as yet to learn what it is to be a Chriftian.   Alas ! you know not with what difpofitions towards each other it was the great defign of my Religion to infpire all who profefs it.

From this paffage we learn what principles it was our Saviour's intention that Chriftians fhould cultivate, and what is the characteriftic badge and glory of his Religion.   We are here taught what it is that peculiarly diftinguifhes a profeffor of the Gofpel from the profeffor of any other Religion, namely, his temper, his difpofition, his fpirit.   *By this fhall all men know that ye are my difciples, if you love one another.*   The Gofpel is a fyftem of benevolence and charity, calculated

culated to infpire men with the kindeft, beft affections towards each o-
ther.

What difpofitions we fhould all acquire, appears from that amiable example our Lord hath exhibited before us in his own conduct. He did
not propagate his Religion in the
world, as fome impoftors have done,
by the dint of force and compulfion,
by conqueft and victory, and obliging
nations of reduced, miferable captives
to embrace his Doctrines. It was not
his defign that any violent meafures
fhould be employed in forcing the
human will, enflaving the human
mind, in laying any cruel embargo
upon our liberty—methods which, inftead of making men fincere converts,
have only made them infincere hypocrites; and inftead of probity and integrity, have only propagated diffi-
mulation and chicane. Read the four
Evan-

Evangelifts, and from the life of Chrift, there plainly recorded, judge whether it was the intention of our divine Inftructor, that fines, imprifonments, confifcations, excommunications, and corporal punifhments, fhould be employed by its profeffors as irrefiftible arguments to refute errour, and eftablifh truth. Read the life of Chrift, and judge whether it was his defign that any fuch infernal court as the Popifh Inquifition fhould ever be erected among Chriftians——that any pecuniary mulcts, any deprivation of property, any penal inflictions, fhould ever take place in order to maintain an unity of Faith, and to keep the peace of his Church unmolefted. Doth the Gofpel, or the life of its Author, give a fanction to any violent, fanguinary methods of promulgating its truths ——forcing men by coercive reftraints to think all alike in matters of Religion——adjufting their opinions to a

2   certain

certain fixed ftandard—obliging them
to refign their underftandings, to refign their liberty—on pain of forfeit-
ing any fecular privileges, on pain of
imprifonment, confifcation, and dif-
grace, embracing fuch a particular
fet of principles—adopting fuch a
number of articles—and fubfcribing
to fuch and fuch a particular creed.
Nothing like this in the Gofpel. The
Gofpel, like its Author, receives all
into its bofom that are holy and fincere, whoever they are. The facrifice, whirh the Gofpel requires, is a
free-will offering. Here there is no
compulfion, except the compulfion of
reafon, argument, and good fenfe.
The evidences in favour of the truth
of the Gofpel are fairly laid before
men, and they are freely left to judge
of their credibility. There are no finifter arts made ufe of to gain converts. Our Saviour wrought his beneficent miracles, and delivered his heavenly

venly Doctrines before vaft crowds, and they were all left to form a judgment of his pretenfions to be a divine Teacher from the proofs he produced. The Miracles and the Doctrines were left to fpeak for themfelves. They carried to every ingenuous, well-difpofed mind their own conviction with them. That man, or that body of men, who ftudy to eftablifh any Religion by worldly emoluments, or punifh the difbelief of it by fecular penalties, may make a number of hypocrites, but can never make a number of converts.

In the Hiftory of the Conqueft of Mexico by Cortez, we read that the priefts of the Spaniards converted five, fix, or ten thoufand Indians every week. A number infinitely greater than what we read of in the Acts of the Apoftles. But what fort of converts were thefe, of whom thefe Spa-
nifh

nish priests boast so extravagantly?—— Not one of them understood a syllable of the Christian Religion, or knew ten words of the Spanish language. But they were baptized by hundreds at a time into the belief of the Christian, I should rather say, of the Popish Religion, and were obliged to embrace the Gospel of which they did not know a word; were obliged to be baptized, or be put to the sword. That was the alternative—— To either the one or the other they must submit——So that by this short and compendious method of conversion the vast and infinitely populous country of Mexico became in a few weeks a Christian country——as wife and rational converts to the Christian Faith as those who had the honour of converting them.

The Gospel is a perfect stranger to such procedures as these. Our Saviour,

P

our, who had all power given him in heaven and in earth, did not exercife his unlimited power in converting the human race to his Religion in this violent, uncontroulable manner. The Gofpel appeals to our reafon—lays its proofs before our underftanding—exhibits its evidences before our minds—and leaves the event with us. If we wilfully reject its evidences, it leaves us, not to the fecular arm, but to the future retributions of the Almighty—If we admit thefe, it leaves us to the rational conviction of our judgment and the confcious approbation of our intellectual powers. The Gofpel difclaims all external reftraint upon the underftanding, all external violence offered to the judgment, leaves men entirely to their moral liberty, leaves them to the operations of their own faculties, would have them the converts of reafon, converts from

principle

principle—such alone will be virtuous, such alone will be sincere.

We find that the Apostles, who were endowed with such miraculous powers and spiritual gifts, did not exercise these amazing endowments in overpowering, in overwhelming mens reason, and forcing them unconvinced into the Christian Church—No, far, far from it—They delivered to them the most excellent and heavenly Doctrines, and left the auditors to reason coolly and deliberately concerning them—They worked miracles, and left the spectators to draw the conclusion.

Would to God their example had ever been followed by those, who have valued themselves upon being their successors. Would to God none had ever usurped any undue dominion in the Christian Church, but had left it to stand upon the solid basis of its in-

trinsic

trinsic excellence, just as our Saviour and his Apostles left it.

But it supplies great, great cause of sincere commiseration, that this blessed Religion, which was designed to unite men to one another in the bonds of harmony, affection, and love, has, by a strange, unnatural perversion, been the very cause of mens irreconcilable enmity and implacable animosity against each other. What a scene of confusion and bloodshed was the Christian Church in the *fourth*, *fifth*, and *sixth* centuries—from the time that Constantine mounted the throne, and interested himself in all the furious, uncharitable disputes that were then agitated. How dreadfully did the Arians and their Opponents retaliate every calamity upon each other by turns, pillaging towns, depopulating countries, massacring with unsparing rage the

i

help-

helpleſs infant and the tender ſex, and wading through feas of blood to eſtabliſh their own particular tenets and ſyſtems of faith.

One, who hath a ſincere value for the honour of the Goſpel, and knows what a mild inſtitution it is, cannot read theſe accounts without horrour —without a mixture of tumultuary paſſions, ſincere pity, and virtuous indignation. When our bleſſed Saviour ſo ſeverely reprehended his two Diſciples for the murderous diſpoſition they diſcovered—to practiſe in the face of the world thoſe very enormities he interdicted—What a proſtitution of the Goſpel is this, what a ſhameful contempt of his plaineſt and beſt admonitions! *A new commandment give I unto you, That ye love one another.*

How

How true have our Saviour's words proved ! *I came not to send peace on the earth, but a sword.* In what age and nation have not these words been fully verified? Have the professors of the Gospel been influenced, are they now influenced, by that mutual affection and love for each other, which are its grand fundamental principles ? Do different denominations of Christians in the present time know, and act as if they knew, what *manner of spirit* the Gospel designed them to be of ? Do different Churches of professing Christians cherish kind, benevolent affections towards each other ; study to promote, though in different ways, the common advancement of the Gospel and the common interests of practical Religion ? Is there less censoriousness, less uncharitableness in the present age than former ages of the Church have seen ? Are professors of the Gospel desirous to cultivate the Christian temper and spirit, to make

the

the life of Chrift the great rule of their
own ; to make all candid, generous
allowances for the different fentiments
of each other ; to give others that liberty of judging, which they claim to
themfelves ?

Alas ! I am afraid we are greatly
departed from the true fpirit of the
Gofpel——I am afraid we have an external form of godlinefs without the
inward power of it. We receive the
grace of God in vain, if we do not
fuffer it to produce its proper fruits
in our hearts and lives. If the Gofpel doth not make us kind in our
difpofitions and charitable in our
judgments, it will be better for us
if we never had been born under its
beams.

Confider what obligations we are
under to cultivate the Chriftian temper and fpirit towards each other. Are
we

we not all frail and fallible ?——Is not
the knowledge of the wifeft of us limited ?——Is not the holinefs of the
beft of us defective ?——Are not our
intellectual faculties clouded and obfcured by neceffary, unavoidable imperfection ?——Are not our improvements in knowledge and virtue few
and inconfiderable ?——Doth not the
intervention of a clay-formed fyftem
clog and impede the operations of our
minds ?——Is not the memory, after
the moft affiduous culture, treache-
rous ?——Is not our boafted reafon in-
volved in a mift of errour and darknefs——not to mention a thoufand prejudices of education, cuftom, and
country, which furround the mind
with their baleful influence, and prevent
it from inveftigating and exploring
truth with unbiaffed freedom and liberal impartiality ? After all our efforts to throw off the incumbent
load of earth and fenfe, ftill we find
morta-

mortality weighs us down. *We see through a glass darkly*—our reasonings are fallacious, our systems imaginary, our opinions prove erroneous, and better acquaintance with books and with men overturns the shadowy fabrics of those fine theories and speculations, which we had vainly erected. Great and good men have erred—the Fathers of the Church have erred—synods and assemblies of learned Divines have erred—How should it be otherwise in this state of imperfection, when different men see the same things in such different lights, and form such different judgments concerning them?

For men to erect themselves to be the supreme standards of infallibility in a state and world so imperfect and erroneous as the present, is both consummate weakness and consummate wickedness—It is impiety against God

P 5 —a

—a fatire upon the Scriptures, which
alone are infallible—an ufurpation of
the rights of confcience, and an inva-
fion of Chriftian freedom and liberty.
Had we judgment and abilities infallibly to decide in all controverfies,
and to determine with clear and accurate precifion in all difputations, we
might then have fome pretenfions for
adjufting the religious tenets of others
to our ftandard.   But fuch an ufurped
dominion over the faith of others is an
undue and unfcriptural claim—and, if
claimed, would only difcover the fhal-
lownefs of our underftanding and the
weaknefs of our judgment—and juftly
expofe us to the derifion and contempt
of the world.   Different educations as
we all refpectively have received—
different prejudices as our minds have
been tinctured with—different princi .
ples as we have been trained up in—
different opportunities for reading and
acquiring knowledge as we have en-

3   joyed

joyed—all thefe are fo many arguments for our exercifing Chriftian
charity and forbearance one towards
another, for making the moft candid
allowances for one another's imperfections, for judging favourably of
each other for their differing from us,
and for our exercifing mutual lenity,
meeknefs, kindnefs, benevolence, and
love towards each other.

Of all men I can truly fay from my
foul, that I pity thofe moft who are
fond of religious difputes—who confider religion in no other view, but
merely as it affords matter for difputation—who read the Word of God,
not fo much to improve their minds
in holinefs, as to furnifh them with
materials for captious controverfies.
Such difputes I am fure have ever
been the bane of practical Religion.
They have been fewel to feed the
flame of unchriftian difcord and un-
christian

chriſtian uncharitableneſs. They have taken mens attention from the great *aim* and *end* of Religion. Vital Religion hath always ſuffered by theſe unhappy diſſenſions — they inducing men to attend more to *words* than *things*—to take up with a *form* of Godlineſs, and pay little regard to the inward *power* of it. I am ſure they damp in the breaſts of Chriſtians that affection and love which is the glory of our Religion, and the perfection of the Goſpel.

It hath ever been my opinion, that we are all agreed in the main fundamental points—that we differ from each other in things by no means eſſential to ſalvation—in things, which he, who diſbelieves, may be as good a Chriſtian, as much an object of the favour of God and Chriſt, as he, who believes them. All Chriſtians of all denominations believe in the Being.
Per-

Perfections, and Government of God
——that his Providence is univerfal——
that we receive all our bleffings and
enjoyments from him——that there is a
future ftate of happinefs or mifery——
that an holy life is indifpenfable to falvation; no happinefs without it——
that the Spirit of God affifts and aids
our infirmities——that Jefus Chrift is
our Redeemer, Saviour, Advocate,
Interceffor, Mediator, and final Judge
——and that we are all purfuing one
and the fame happinefs——all agree in
thefe fundamental points of Chriftian Religion——and who does not fee
that all other points are, comparatively, trivial, frivolous, and indiffe-
rent?

With regard to myfelf, I lay no
ftrefs at all upon any particular fpeculative opinions of my own; and
fhould deteft myfelf if I thought any
man a worfe Chriftian, merely becaufe
he

he differs from me. The only thing I lay infinite ftrefs upon, is the advancement of Holinefs and the Chriftian temper both in myfelf and others, the improvement of my own mind, and the minds of you, my hearers, in the practical truths of the Gofpel. A good life and converfation is the furn and fubftance of Religion—a heart full of love to God, to Jefus Chrift, and to all our fellow Chriftians—walking before our families and the world in fuch a manner as to pleafe God and fecure his bleffing—keeping our tempers and fpirits under good government—mortifying our corrupt affections—labouring to correct what is amifs in our tempers and affections—living awfully mindful of God's prefence with us—ftudying to promote the glory of God—making the Scriptures our ftudy and comfort in this tranfient ftate of our pilgrimage—ftriving to know the Will of God,

that

that we may conform to it—and by
the regular courſe of an amiable, uſeful, charitable life, making the beſt
preparation we are able for the hour
of death, and our happy entrance into a better world. I would rather
write ten pages to promote mens attention to theſe great, practical, vital,
ſaving Truths, than ten thouſand volumes of the moſt learned and elaborate Controverſy the Republic of Theology ever ſaw,

Alas! thoſe who delight in ſouring
their own minds and the minds of
others with theſe unhappy, unedify-
ing conteſts, *know not what manner of
ſpirit they are of*, are unhappy ſtrangers
to the genius and ſpirit of the Goſpel,
and are yet to learn in what the true
dignity and glory of it conſiſts.

If I underſtand the New Teſtament
after ſeveral years intenſe ſtudy and
impar-

Impartial examination of it, with prayer to God to aſſiſt my imperfect mind in its enquiries, I am fully convinced it was never deſigned to fill our heads with uſeleſs ſpeculations, but our hearts with practical principles——to make us good parents, good heads of families, good children, good neighbours, good members of ſociety ——to inſpire us with the love of God and our bleſſed Redeemer——to make us uſeful to one another in this tranſitory ſcene of mortality——to fill us with joy and hope in believing——and by a holy life and a blameleſs converſation to engage us to prepare for that bleſſed world which it reveals.   O what animating truths are theſe !——what encouraging, comforting, practical doctrines are theſe, worth all the uſeleſs loads of uſeleſs controverſy that ever were written.   Who, that believes theſe Truths, and acts ſuitably to ſuch a belief, would not be powerfully

fully engaged to cherish the kindest affections towards all his fellow Christians, view them, together with himself, as blessed with the same evangelical privileges, as equally conversant with himself in the same vale of frailty and mortality, as endowed with immortal souls by the distinguishing privileges of their birth, and as swiftly travelling with him, and not in very different roads, through a vain, momentary scene, to those blessed abodes where sin and sorrow never enter. *He that hath this hope in him purifieth himself, even as he is pure.* Who would not, that hath these prospects, all this consummate happiness in view, study to bring his spirit under proper discipline, to regulate all his affections, to cherish and exercise the most benevolent dispositions, and by consulting the peace and tranquillity of his own mind, and the concord, unanimity, and

and happiness of those around him, prepare for that blessed world, where universal harmony reigns among all its various and innumerable inhabitants.

F I N I S.

Just published,

By JOSEPH JOHNSON, *No. 72, St. Paul's Church-yard, in Two Volumes, 120, Price Seven Shillings bound,*

Η   ΚΑΙΝΗ   ΔΙΑΘΗΚΗ.

THE NEW TESTAMENT, collated with the moſt approved Manuſcripts : with ſelect Notes in Engliſh, Critical and Explanatory ; and References to thoſe Authors who have beſt illuſtrated the Sacred Writings. To which are added, A Catalogue of the principal Editions of the Greek Teſtament ; and a Liſt of the moſt eſteemed Commentators and Critics.

By E. HARWOOD, D. D.

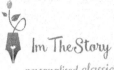